SCIENTIFIC EDITOR: Anthoula Tsaroucha

Editor: Andreas Bayias
Translation: William Phelps
Plans and Maps: Dimos Svolopoulos
Cover Design: R.V. Graphics
Photography: D. Benetos, M. Skiadaresis
DTP: Spyridoula Vonitsi

1, Diad. Pavlou St., 154 52 Psychico, Athens
tel./ fax 210-6719868, 210-3475012

ISBN: 960-89242-7-8

Printed and bound in Greece

The plans on pages 20 and 35 are based on those of G. Roux and J. Pouilloux

DELPHI

MONUMENTS AND MUSEUM

BY PROFESSOR PHOTIOS PETSAS
Former Director of Antiquities at Delphi

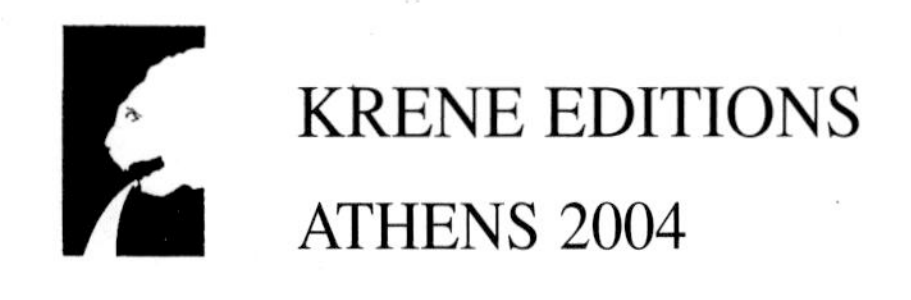

KRENE EDITIONS
ATHENS 2004

"And as soon as we reached the base of the two Phaidriades, we found ourselves facing what seemed like the chasm of all chasms: the two cliffs divided by a tremendous gorge, narrow and impassable... There, in the depths of the gorge, where the two cliffs united, a crystalline stream gushed forth abruptly, the stream of Kastalia, the famed spring in which they all, priests and votaries, washed themselves before entering the temple..."

Chr. Karouzos

▲ *Apollo depicted inside a kylix (N. Sigalas).*

◀ *Kastalian Spring in 1833 (J. M. Wittmer: Benaki Museum).*

THE SITE AND THE CULT OF APOLLO

The Site

A remote place, richly endowed by nature, Delphi, became a sacred place from earliest antiquity, then a refuge for the mariners who eventually became its priests and, finally, a cross-roads and the navel (omphalos) of the earth.

Delphi was in ancient Phocis, but this does not correspond exactly to the district of present day Phocis, as considerable parts of the ancient Phocis now belong to the districts of Boeotia and Phthiotis. Ancient Phocis included about twenty settlements, of which Delphi was the most important, because the Sanctuary of Apollo was within its boundaries. The mountains of Phocis include the many summits of Parnassos in the centre (H.2459 m), the lower and flatter Kirphys in the south and their foothills. Among these mountains lie small plains, watered by the streams of the Rivers Kephissos and Pleistos (the ancient Phocians would have used the plains for winter quarters and the mountains for the summer). The gorge of the Pleistos is the main approach to Delphi from the Gulf of Corinth through the pass of present day Itea, which was Kirrha, the port of Delphi in antiquity. An approach from the east leads through the pass of Arachova from Thebes, Chaeronea and Levadia while a third approach comes down between the mountains of Parnassos and Gkiona through Amphissa. There are also roads from the west. Thus, when the sanctuary at Delphi attained importance it became a real cross-roads and was, therefore, called the navel of the earth.

The site, which lies at an altitude of 500-700 m, is dominated by the cliffs of the Phaidriades, between which runs the Kastalian Spring, whose waters first gave Delphi its importance. The panoramic view from the site encompasses the sheer grey-green sides of Mt Kirphys, the gorge of the Pleistos running through the plain of Amphissa and Itea, the sea of ancient Kirrha and, beyond it, the Gulf of Corinth and the endless mountains of the Peloponnese. It is a marvellous view of great natural beauty, to which the vast silver-green olive groves have been added by man.

The Prehistory

In remotest antiquity the site was perhaps of only limited importance; as far as is known man was only present from the third millennium BC. The first settlement was on the coast in the bay of Kirrha (or Krisa) and lasted from the beginning of the Bronze Age down to Mycenaean times, but after 1600 BC a higher settlement further inland attained importance, near the present day Chryso, which is identified with Krisa of historical times. Higher still a small plain with an acropolis called Lycoreia, near the Corycian Cave, was also inhabited in the Bronze Age. In Mycenaean times, from at least 1400 BC, Delphi, the "rocky Pytho" of Homer, was the sanctuary of a female deity, Ge or Athena, who gave oracles through a prophetess. Other gods probably worshipped, were Poseidon and Dionysus while, later, sacred rocks also received some kind of cult (the Omphalos, the Stone of Kronos), as did the

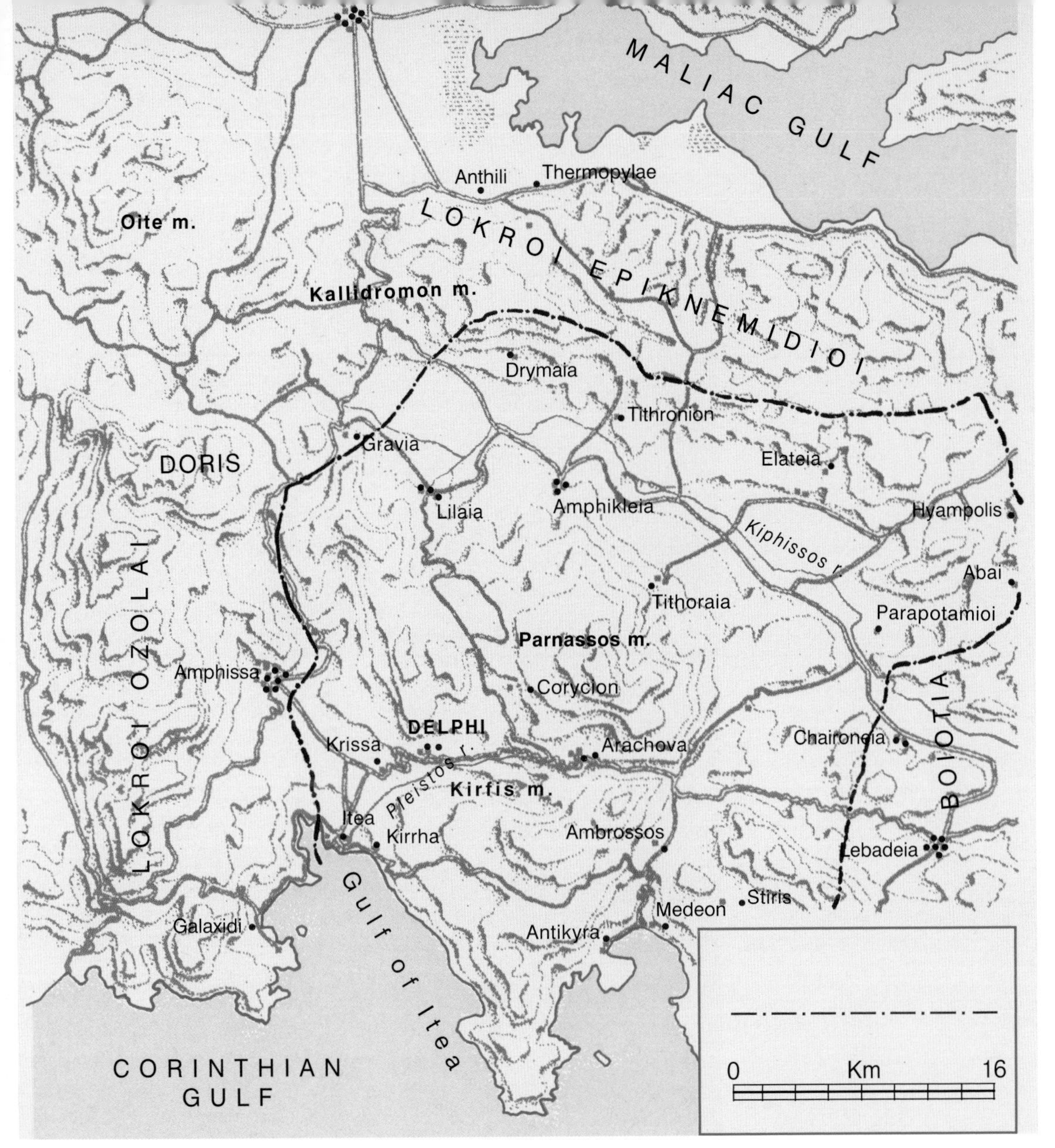

Map of ancient Phocis.

hero Pyrrhos or Neoptolemos. Mycenaean Delphi was destroyed by a rock fall towards the end of the Bronze Age.

Early Historical Times

Delphi prospered again in the 8th century BC and the first information about the Apollo cult belongs to this period. In the first lines of the play "The Eumenides" by Aeschylus (458 BC) the Pythia relates that Ge (or Gaia), the mother of the gods and the first prophetess, was succeeded by her daughters, Themis and then the Titan, Phoebe, who gave her name to Phoebus Apollo. The complete myth, or a

Panoramic view of the Delphic landscape from NE.

variation of it, is preserved in the so-called Homeric Hymn to Pythian Apollo (7th century BC). According to this Hymn Apollo built his first temple in a wooded grove at Delphi and became the first male possessor of the site, having killed the Pytho, a female serpent who guarded the prophetic spring of Kassotis. To purify himself of this crime Apollo went to the Vale of Tempe, from whence he brought the laurel with which he built the first temple. He gave oracles in the shrine of Ge through a Pythia, who sat bound at the mouth of a chasm in the earth from which 'vapours' arose. The first priests of Apollo were Cretans from Knossos, whom Apollo, in the guise of a dolphin, drove to Kirrha after a wandering sea voyage. The mariners asked the god how they could survive in such a barren place and he replied that they would live effortlessly from the offerings of his worshippers. The Cretan priests introduced the worship of Apollo Delphinios (the Dolphin) to Delphi and brought with them a very old wooden idol (xoanon), and perhaps changed the name of the Pytho to that of Delphi.

In the mid-8th century BC the brothers Trophonios and Agamedes, sons of Erginos, who were famous for other exploits, built the first ashlar masonry temple. The oracle gained a great reputation not only in Greece but through all the then known world. Greek cities and private citizens as well as foreign kings consulted it and offered rich gifts. There is a myth that Zeus, wishing to find the centre of the earth, freed an eagle at each end of the world and that they met at Delphi, which thus gained the reputation of the 'navel of the earth'; an omphalos (navel stone) became one of its holy emblems.

The wealth accumulated by Delphi aroused the envy of Kirrha (Krisa), who then taxed the visiting worshippers. This caused the First Sacred War (595-586 BC) waged by the Amphictyonic League against Kirrha, which was destroyed in 590 BC.

The Amphictyonic League

This was composed of twelve tribes from Central Greece, Attica, Euboea and the north-east Peloponnese and had its centre initially at the shrine of Demeter at Anthele near Thermopylae; they were the Ainianes, Achaians, Phthiotians, Dolopes, Dorians, Thessalians, Ionians, Lokrians, Malians, Magnetes, Perrhaibians and Phocians. Their representatives, of which there were two per tribe, called Ieromnemones, did not represent their cities but their tribes. If necessary, the so-called Pylagorai could be sent to Thermopylae and a general assembly could also be called which was open to all the citizens of the cities in the League. In the 7th century BC the League decided that Delphi should become its second centre and, after that, they met every spring (in the month of Bysios) at Anthele and every autumn (in the month of Boukatios) at Delphi. It was the fate of the sanctuary to be involved in three more Sacred Wars, making a total of four in 250 years. The priests of Apollo did not play a passive role in these events and, as the oracle was the hub of the Greek and foreign world, they had enormous influence.

The Amphictyonic League organised the Pythian Games and administered the sanctuary acting with the people of Delphi. The people probably had an oligarchic government as only the leaders had political rights. Every year probably nine prytaneis (rectors) were chosen, one of whom was the eponymous archon. A council of six members was chosen every six months and the rulling body was a popular assembly. The Delphians appointed the Pythia, the two priests of Apollo, two "prophets" and five "holy men". It collected the price for each oracle (pelanos), granted the privilege of promanteia (precedence in consulting the oracle) and saw to the general organisation.

The Oracle

The Oracle of Dodona was honoured as the oldest of the great panhellenic sanctuaries and Olympia was very well-known because of the Olympian Games, but no sanctuary surpassed Delphi in reputation and wealth, owing to its oracle and games. Although the ancient authors give much information about the oracle, many problems unfortunately still remain concerning its character and procedure.

Everything in Greece has a mythological origin. Parnassos, the eponymous hero of Mount Parnassos, was said to be the first to prophesy from bird flight: thus this kind of prophesy probably began in a place with much bird life. Another legend says that Delphos, the eponymous hero of Delphi, was the first to read entrails, while Amphictyon, the eponymous hero of the Amphictyonic League, was the first to interpret dreams. The so-called Pyrkooi prophesied from the flames of the sacred fire at Delphi. Elsewhere in Greece the pebbles used for prophesy were called Thriai, but at Delphi mythology says the Thriai were nymphs who actually prophesied. Myth and tradition show clearly that every method of prophesy, such as birds, entrails, dreams and pebbles, was known at Delphi.

The famous Delphic Oracle, however, owed its reputation equally to another form of prophesy: Apollo himself spoke through the Pythia. Originally the Oracle spoke only once a year, probably when Apollo's birthday was celebrated on the 7th day of Bysios (Feb-Mar). From the 6th century BC onwards, as patronage increased, the Oracle prophesied on the 7th day of every month, except for the three winter months when Apollo went to the Hyperboreans and left the sanctuary in the hands of Dionysos: thus, the calm god of light gave up his sanctuary to the god of wine and revelry, who had his own temple next to that of Apollo.

The Pythia was a woman over fifty who left her family to enter the service of Apollo and lived in a special dwelling in the sanctuary so that she should remain pure. She wore virgin white in spite of her age and followed certain holy precepts. It was not necessary that she be beautiful or of good family. Initially there was only one Pythia, but, as the reputation and patronage of the Oracle increased, two more were added. This was still not enough, so the privilege of promanteia can be readily appreciated. This was given by the Delphians to cities and private citizens along with other privileges such as proxenia (the official representation of a city) and asylia (immunity). Cities who had a representative at Delphi could consult the Oracle on any day, if the god was

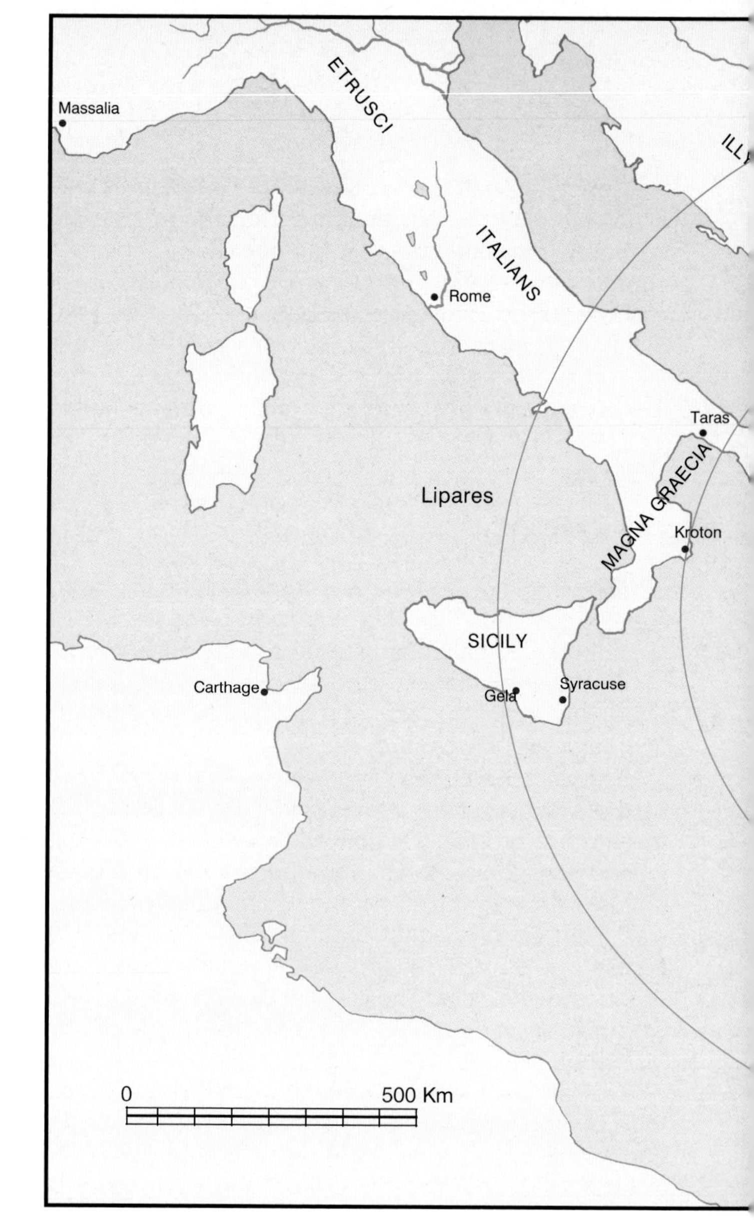

Delphi in the centre of the ancient world with the principal cities that consulted the Oracle and built or sent the most important votive offerings.

willing. To ascertain this a goat was sacrificed but was first sprinkled with cold water; if it shivered, the god had no objection.

A suppliant first paid the pelanos and provided animals for the sacrifice and for the sacred table. He drew lots for order of preference. On the morning of the day of prophesy the Pythia would go to the Kastalian Spring at daybreak to purify herself. She would drink from the other sacred spring, Kassotis, and chew laurel. The priests, who had also washed in Kastalia, ceremoniously escorted the Pythia to the inner shrine (adyton) of the temple. The sacred tripod, the chair of Apollo, was supposed to be here and the Pythia would sit on it, thus taking the place of the god. The tripod was by the mouth of the chasm, the site of the omphalos, the grave of Dionysos and the gold statue of Apollo. The suppliant would also be ceremoniously escorted to the inner

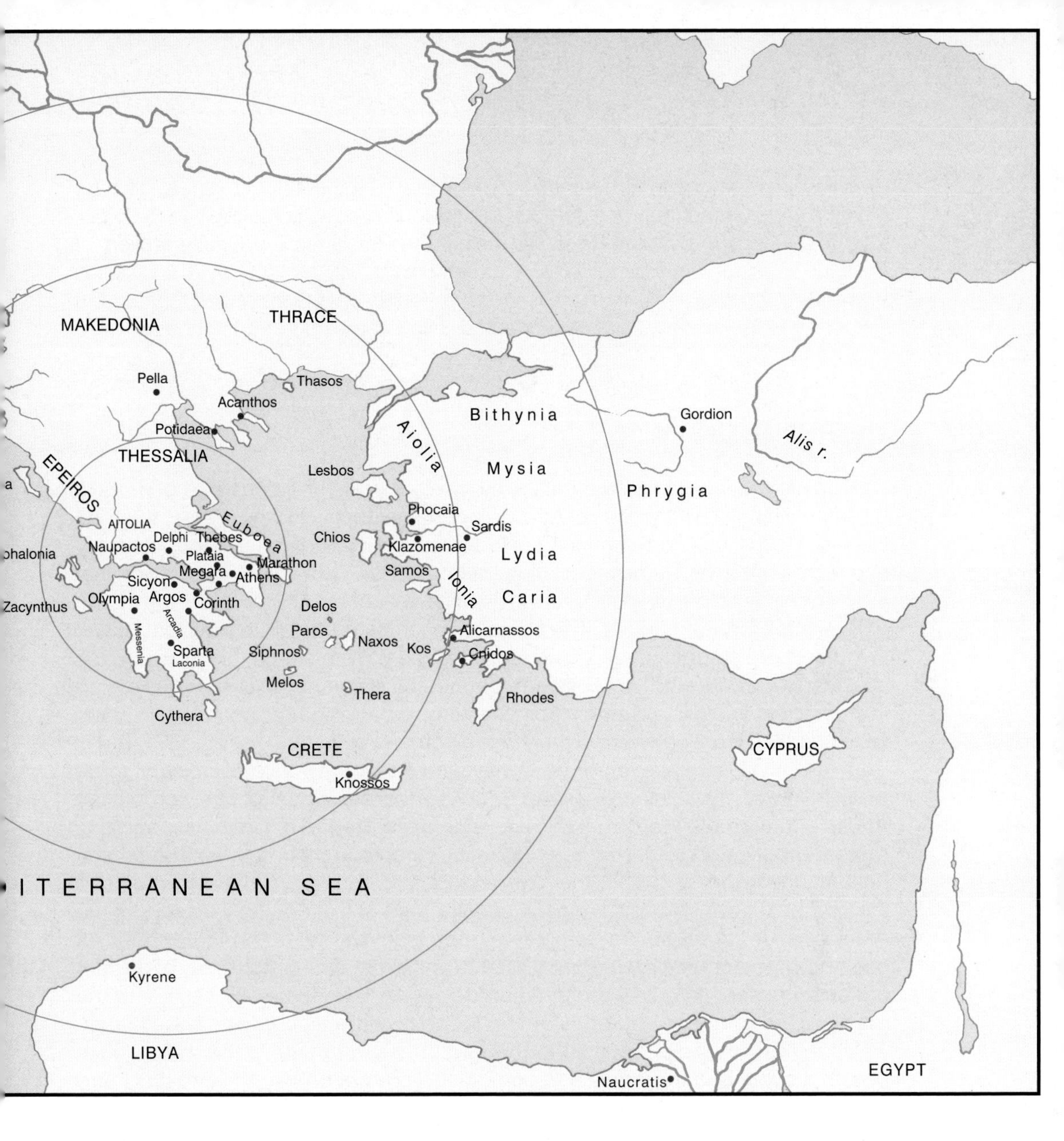

shrine and put in a special seat, without seeing the Pythia, who was separated by a curtain. Meanwhile the priests had prepared the sacrifice and lit the fire on the great altar (a gift from Chios). City representatives and private individuals assembled piously round the altar outside the temple and awaited their turn. First the Delphians consulted the Oracle, then those who had the privilege of promanteia and finally everyone else, in an order determined by lot.

The suppliants put their question, written or oral, through one of the priests who read it to the Pythia, who was out of sight and hypnotised from chewing laurel leaves, and from the incense and smoke. She replied in incoherent words and incomprehensible shouts which the priests interpreted into hexameters and the suppliant took this written answer with him. The answer, which was ambiguous, was interpreted by the suppliant as it pleased him and, only if the future turned out otherwise, did he see the true answer. This explains the epithet Loxian Apollo, the Oblique One. One of the most famous ambiguous oracles is the reply to Croesus, king of Lydia, who asked if he would defeat the Persians. The Oracle replied, 'If Croesus crosses the River Halys, a great power will be destroyed'. Croesus interpreted the oracle in his favour, crossed the River Halys between Lydia and Persia with a great army and was defeated. The Oracle had been right again.

The Pythian Games

Originally these Games took place every eight years and consisted of musical contests with poetic hymns to Apollo accompanied by the lyre. After the First Sacred War the Amphictyonic League took over the management of the sanctuary and reorganised the Games, enriching them with new contests and arranging that they should be held every four years in the third year of the Olympiads in the month of Boukatios (end of August). The prizes were laurel crowns from the oldest laurel in the Vale of Tempe and the victors obtained the right to set up their statue in the sanctuary. A truce was announced three months beforehand all over Greece so that participants could assemble from the furthest parts and get home again. Each state sent a delegation who were named theoroi (watchers).

The festival lasted seven days. On the first day there was a sacrifice of three bulls followed by a sacred drama showing the slaughter of the serpent by Apollo. Plutarch mentions that this was called the Stepteria. On the second day a great procession took place in which the priests in their rich vestments, the delegations from the states, the competitors, etc. took part, all bearing gifts to the god. It set out from the Halos, a circular area in front of the Treasury of the Athenians. In front of the temple a huge sacrifice of a hundred bulls (a hecatomb) took place on the great altar from Chios. On the third day at a great banquet the sacrifices of the preceding day were ceremoniously eaten and the power of the god thus imbibed. On the fourth day drama contests were held in which hymns to Apollo were performed with the lyre or flute, either by a soloist or with a choir, and tragedies and comedies were put on. On the fifth day there were contests in the stadium. The dolichos (long distance race) was twelve courses of the stadium, the stadion was a race of one stade (178.35 m) while the diaulos was a race of two stades. The pentathlon consisted of five contests (running, wrestling, jumping, throwing the discus and the javelin) and there were also separate wrestling and boxing contests, a pankration, which was a combination of boxing and wrestling, and finally a race of men under arms. The Amphictyonic League introduced the chariot race with two and four horse chariots. These races occurred in the hippodrome on the sixth day while the gymnastic contests were on the seventh day and, as one day was often not sufficient, they took an extra day so that the contests lasted eight days in all. The Pythian Games differed from the other panhellenic games because they included contests with religious hymns accompanied by the lyre and flute. Music in a broader sense than that on today (ie. including the associated arts) was the especial love of Apollo.

The Reputation of the Oracle and the Treasuries

From the 8th century BC onwards and especially in the Archaic Period, the reputation of the Oracle spread through all the then known world and Greeks and foreigners consulted it, the Greeks especially before founding a colony, as Apollo was considered the archigetes (founder) of colonies; indeed there are many called Apollonia after him. Syracuse and Croton in Magna Craecia, Cyrene in Africa and Thasos in the north Aegean are some of the more important colonies who held Delphic Apollo as their protector. The mythical king of Phrygia, Midas, sent his throne to the sanctuary at the beginning of the 7th century BC, from far off Gordion in the heart of Asia Minor, to show his piety to Apollo. Another king, Gyges of Lydia, ancestor of Croesus, sent gold kraters, silver offerings and pure gold from Sardis about 675 BC. In Greece, the tyrant Kypselus of Corinth, who was renowned for his wealth, built the first treasury at Delphi and other leaders and cities followed his example. These small buildings, constructed on a temple plan, multiplied to decorate the sanctuary and cover the smaller precious offerings. In the mid-6th century BC a descendant of Gyges, Croesus, king of Lydia, consulted the Oracle because he had been assured of its supremacy before attacking the Persians (see above) and sent many rich gifts. Among other gold and silver offerings was a pure gold lion weighing 250 kilos set on a pyramid of 117 blocks of white gold (an amalgam of gold and silver). Two huge kraters, one gold and one silver were put each side of the temple entrance. Croesus, Amasis of Egypt and the Greeks themselves put large sums towards the construction of a new larger temple after the destruction of the earlier one by fire in 548 BC. It cost 300 talents (hundreds of thousands of drachmas). The Alcmaeonids, exiled from Athens by the Peisistratids at this time, took over the work of reconstruction and paid out of their own pocket to put Parian marble in the facade instead of the cheaper poros which the contract specified.

The Classical Period (5th and 4th centuries BC)

During the Persian War in 480 BC Delphi was saved from attack by the miraculous intervention of Apollo. A huge rock tumbled down from the Phaidriades and the Persians fled panic stricken. This famous victory by relatively few Greeks over thousands of Persians was attributed by the pious victors to the help of Apollo, and perhaps not unjustly, because training for the Games was a part of Greek religion, as is mentioned in the Homeric Hymn to Apollo Delios: "The Ionians with their long chitons assemble to honour you and... in each contest they entertain you, Apollo, with boxing and dancing and singing". The results of training body and mind appeared in the contest for freedom. E. N. Gardiner observes, "The victory of the Greeks over the Persians... was the victory of a handful of trained athletes against hordes of soft barbarians".

The Athenians, the greatest victors of the Persian War, dedicated the famous Treasury of the Athenians and the Stoa of the Athenians to Apollo after their victory of the Battle of Marathon. Other Greeks made equally brilliant gifts. A colossal statue of Apollo was set up after the sea-battle of Salamis and a wonderful golden tripod after the Battle of Plataea, inscribed with the names of the thirty-one Greek cities who defeated the army of the Great King. Delphi now began to mint silver coins.

In the mid-5th century BC the Phocians took over the sanctuary with Athenian help. This caused the Second Sacred War, 448-446 BC, ending in the return of the sanctuary to the Delphians with Spartan help. In 373 BC the Temple of Apollo was destroyed when huge rocks fell on it as the result of an earthquake. Its reconstruction began immediately under the supervision of naopes and the cost was met by the Delphians and the Amphictyonic League with a special tax per head (epikephalos obolos) and also by the rest of Greece. The calculations and costs are inscribed on a marble stele (on show in the Museum). However, the reconstruction of the temple was interrupted by a new Sacred War.

The Third Sacred War, 356-346 BC, arose from the eternal strife between the Delphians and the other Phocians. The latter occupied the sanctuary again for about ten years, seized the revenues and melted down the precious offerings. The rest of Greece was horrified and Philip II of Macedon took the opportunity to intervene, with the result that the Phocians were defeated, ejected from the Amphictyonic League and compelled to pay a fine of 420 talents.

The Fourth Sacred War, 340-338 BC, was against the Locrians of Amphissa and ended in Philip of Macedon strengthening his hold on Greece after the Battle of Chaeronea, 338 BC, and taking over the two Phocian votes in the Amphictyonic League. At his instigation Delphi now minted silver staters which showed Apollo on the omphalos on one side and Demeter on the other.

The prosperity of Delphi did not suffer much during the two 4th century Sacred Wars; on the contrary this century was still a golden age for the growth of the sanctuary. During this period the new temple of Athena Pronaia was built as well as the Tholos, the Gymnasium, the Treasuries of Thebes and Cyrene, the Stadium, etc.

The Hellenistic Period

The structure of the Greek world was radically altered under the Macedonian kings. Instead of city-states, the Amphictyonic League, colonies, allies, etc., the Hellenistic period is characterised by large kingdoms. The Greeks had widened man's horizons with poetry, philosophy, drama, etc., but Alexander the Great had widened the horizons of the world. Thus he created a unified cultural area, where the old beliefs warred with the new political conditions and fused into new religious and philosophical conceptions. The great sanctuaries of the Hellenistic world were now centres of dynastic propaganda. Outside the large kingdoms some traditional institutions continued their life.

One of these institutions, the Aetolian League, gained prestige by a victory over the Galatians who were attacking Delphi which, with the miraculous help of Apollo, was saved again, but now the Aetolians were the new masters of the sanctuary and inaugurated a yearly festival, the Salvation Festival, to preserve the memory on their great victory. They dedicated their Galatian plunder in their huge stoa outside and immediately west of the sanctuary. The kings of Pergamon showed their respect to Apollo.

After his victory over the Galatians in Asia Minor, Attalos I gave many gifts, including a stoa with paintings, scores of statues, an "oikos", a covered exedra, etc... Eumenes II and Attalos II gave large sums to learning and the arts, to the completion of the theatre and to the organisation of the festivals, the Eumeneia and the Attaleia.

The Attalids also took care to set up their statues in a prominent position in the sanctuary.

The most famous of the Macedonian gifts is the offering of Krateros. Perseus, the last king of Macedon, was preparing to set up his statue on a high column in front of the temple but, after his defeat by the Roman general, Aemilius Paulus, at Pydna in 168 BC, the victor set up his own equestrian statue on the same column. The Romans had become masters of the sanctuary in 191 BC and introduced the Roman pantheon and their own festival.

Delphi under the Romans

The nominal protection of Rome was not sufficient to protect Delphi form voracious plundering, even at the hands of the emperors themselves. It was plundered by the Maidoi of Thrace one winter and in 86 BC Sulla seized all the remaining precious offerings, which had survived so many centuries. The Maidoi burnt the temple and, for the first time in hundreds of years, the holy flame in the shrine went out.

Augustus took the sanctuary under his protection again, re-organised the Amphictyonic League and initiated the worship of the emperors in the Tholos in the Pronaia. Nevertheless, the city of Delphi was gradually deserted. Later Nero carried off five hundred statues but, on the other hand, Domitian repaired the temple. Plutarch spent more than twenty years at Delphi (105-126 AD) as a priest of Apollo and tried to resurrect the ancient cult. Hadrian and Antoninus later did the same. Herodes Atticus included Delphi in his generosity, setting up stone seats in the Stadium, not marble ones, as Pausanias noted on his visit to Delphi in 170 AD, when he found the sanctuary neglected, but still rich in treasuries and works of art. Enough remained to be taken later to Constantinople by Constantine the Great and Theodosius. The Edict of Jan. 10, 381 AD struck the last blow at the worship of Apollo and the ancient religious tradition gave way to Christianity. According to legend, when Julian the Apostate sent Oreibasios to consult the Oracle, the Pythia gave her last melancholy utterance, a funeral epigram to the old religion:

Tell the king, the fair-wrought hall has fallen to the ground.
No longer has Phoebus a hut, nor a prophetic laurel,
Nor a spring that speaks. The water of speech even is quenched.

(Translation by H.W. Parke, The Delphic Oracle)

THE MONUMENTS*

The Recent Archaeological History of the Site

Delphi did not cease to live in one sense or another in Byzantine and later times. The monastery of the Dormition of the Virgin, where the English traveller Edward Dodwell was offered hospitality, was on top of the ruined palaestra in the Gymnasium. It was removed by the French for their excavations, as were also the churches of St. John and St. George near the Apollo Temple. Most of the area of the sanctuary was taken up by the village of Kastri, which was also moved to its present position and renamed Delphi. From 150 AD onwards travellers called at Delphi, historians and archaeologists of every nationality, such as Cyriacus of Ancona (1436), Spon and Wheler (1676), Chandler (1766), Dodwell (1805), Holland (1812) and Gell (1819). Important information was noted by the Englishman W.M.Leake (1806) and the Germans, Thiersch (1840) and Ulrichs, who became a professor at Athens University.

One of the first to start excavating was the German K. Otfrid Müller with his student Ernst Curtius. In 1860 the Frenchmen, Wescher and Foucart, investigated the polygonal retaining wall and published inscriptions found in the basements and courtyards of the old village. Twenty years later the Frenchman Haussoulier uncovered part of the Stoa of the Athenians and, in 1887, the German Pomtow excavated the entrance to the sanctuary and carried out important topographical research. The interest of the Archaeological Service of the then newly constituted state of Greece was manifested from 1861, and in 1870, after an earthquake had destroyed the old village, efforts began to move it to a new site. Greek archaeologists (Dragoumis and Kastorchis) dug the site of Kastalia. The Americans and Germans sought permission to excavate the whole site but eventually it was granted to the French School of Archaeology in Athens in 1891 under the directorship of Théophile Homolle and systematic excavations began in 1892, together with the removal of the village. The results of the excavations are mostly published in the journal of the French School, the Bulletin de Correspondance Hellénique and in the volumes of the series Fouilles de Delphes. Among the Greek archaeologists who have worked at Delphi the unforgettable Anthony Keramopoullos and Christos Karouzos (whose mother came from Delphi) rendered important services before the Second World War, when the archaeological office for the area was at Thebes. The author was the first Ephor of Antiquities to have his headquarters at Delphi in 1944. He concentrated on rescue work, as did Alexander Kondoleon, who died in April 1942, so that the antiquities and the Museum were spared the ravages of war and occupation.

The large archaelogical site of Delphi is divided in two by the Spring of Kastalia: to the east is the Sanctuary of Athena Pronaia, the Gymnasium, the east cemetery, etc.; to the west is the Sanctuary of Apollo, the Stadium, the

---

** The black numbers in parentheses refer to the corresponding plans of the Sanctuary of Athena Pronaia, the Gymnasium, the Sanctuary of Apollo, and to all the other monuments included on the fold-out plan of the Sanctuary at the end of the book.*

View of the ancient site of Delphi West of the Kastalian Spring from NE. ▶

ruins of the city, the west cemetery, etc.. The Sanctuary of Athena Pronaia, situated before the Apollo Temple, was the first sanctuary the ancient visitor came to and so received its name "Pronaia" (before the temple). Pausanias, the 2nd century AD traveller, begins his description of Delphi from the Pronaia Sanctuary (Pausanias, *Guide to Greece* X. 8.6).

The Sanctuary of Athena Pronaia

The usual name for the area is Marmaria (the Marbles) because of the ancient marble remains. It is a sloping area which was terraced in antiquity. The earliest remains are Mycenaean: clay female figurines (on show in the Museum) perhaps come from the shrine of a female deity, a predecessor of Athena.

The ancient east entrance is now closed and it is necessary to descend from the direction of Kastalia by a winding path, before reaching the east end of the sanctuary where the tour begins, as it did in antiquity.

Pausanias first noted the more important shrines in the sanctuary, which were still preserved in his time, and then recalls the shrine there of the hero Phylacos, who, according to legend, took part in the war against the Persians. He fought at the side of another hero, Autonoos, who had a shrine near Kastalia under Hyampeia, as Herodotus recounts. The two heroes amazed the Persians by their gigantic stature and thus put them to flight. Starting at the northwest entrance of the Pronaia Sanctuary there are two buildings **(1-2)** built on a temple plan, that is with a pronaos (vestibule) and a sekos (inner room). Only the polygonal stone foundations are preserved. The dimensions of the smaller are 4.85 by 3.95 m, the larger 6.10 by 8 m. They lie on a higher terrace between retaining walls and are entered from the south. It was thought that this was the

Plan of the sanctuary of Athena Pronaia: **1-2.** *Archaic temple-shaped treasuries.* **3.** *Archaic temple of Athena Pronaia.* **4.** *Doric Treasury.* **5.** *Ionic Treasury of the Massaliots.* **6.** *Tholos.* **7.** *Later Temple of Athena Pronaia.* **8.** *"House of the Priests".* **9.** *Base of a trophy.*

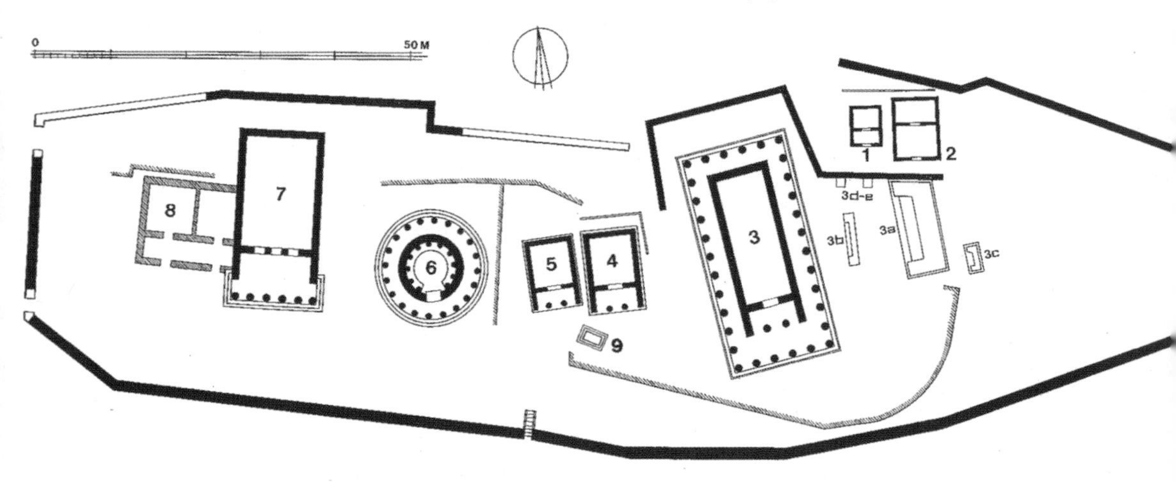

View of the ruins in the enclosure of Athena Pronaia from E.

shrine of Phylacos, but, because of their likeness to the Treasuries **(4-5)** (for example the similar layout, dimensions and positions, with the smaller behind the larger), it is now thought that they were probably treasuries, which were abandoned for some reason and replaced by the two more ornate ones **(4-5)**.

The area between the two pairs of temples is, as is known today, the most ancient sacred place in Marmaria. Remains of Mycenaean worship were found here and it was here too that one of the oldest and most magnificent Greek temples was built for Athena in about 650 BC. It was a poros peripteral in the Doric order. Twelve of its capitals, of the earliest known Doric architecture, and parts of its columns were in the foundations of the second Archaic temple, which was built on top of it. They are now lined up on the west side.

The Second Archaic Temple **(3)** was built about 500 BC. It is a large peripteral temple also in the Doric order (27.45 by 13.25 m), whose plan was dictated by the narrowness of its site so that the columns on the ends are only half the number of those on the long sides, ie. 6 by 12. The pronaos is composed of two columns *in antis* (between pilasters). There was no opisthodomos (back chamber) behind the sekos as there was no room. The temple was damaged in the Persian War and also in the earthquake in 373 BC. The three columns which are still preserved at the south-east corner have 4th century BC isodomic strengthening walls between them, probably built after the earthquake. In March 1905 torrential rains caused a rockfall from Hyampeia which destroyed ten of the then remaining columns. In 1977 the Greek Archaeological Service used special technicians and broke and removed these rocks. The preserved pedimental and metope sculptures are kept in the Museum.

To the east of the Athena Temple are the remains of a large rectangular altar **(3a)** of the 6th century BC, which is thought to have functioned as an altar in the Sanctuary, and which has a smaller altar on each of its long sides **(3b-c)**. Between the altars **3a** and **3c** are three upright stelai, perhaps belonging to three offering tables (altars), dedicated, according to the inscriptions, to *Zeus Polieus, Athena Ergane and Athena Zosteria.* The first inscription was found by A. Keramopoullos south of the temple in 1907. Two other built altars on the retaining wall belong to the goddesses *Hygeia* and *Eileithyia* **(3d-e)**, according to the inscriptions on the wall.

After a glance at the well-built retaining walls the visitor should proceed to the treasuries **(4-5)** which are built of Parian marble. The larger, the Doric Treasury, (7.30 by 10.40 m) has two columns *in antis* and was built immediately after the Persian War. The smaller, the Massaliote Treasury, which is in the Ionic order (6.37 by 8.63 m) and considered slightly older, equalled the Siphnian Treasury in the Apollo Sanctuary in beauty. The two columns *in antis* have "aeolic", capitals decorated with palm leaves. Small parts of the

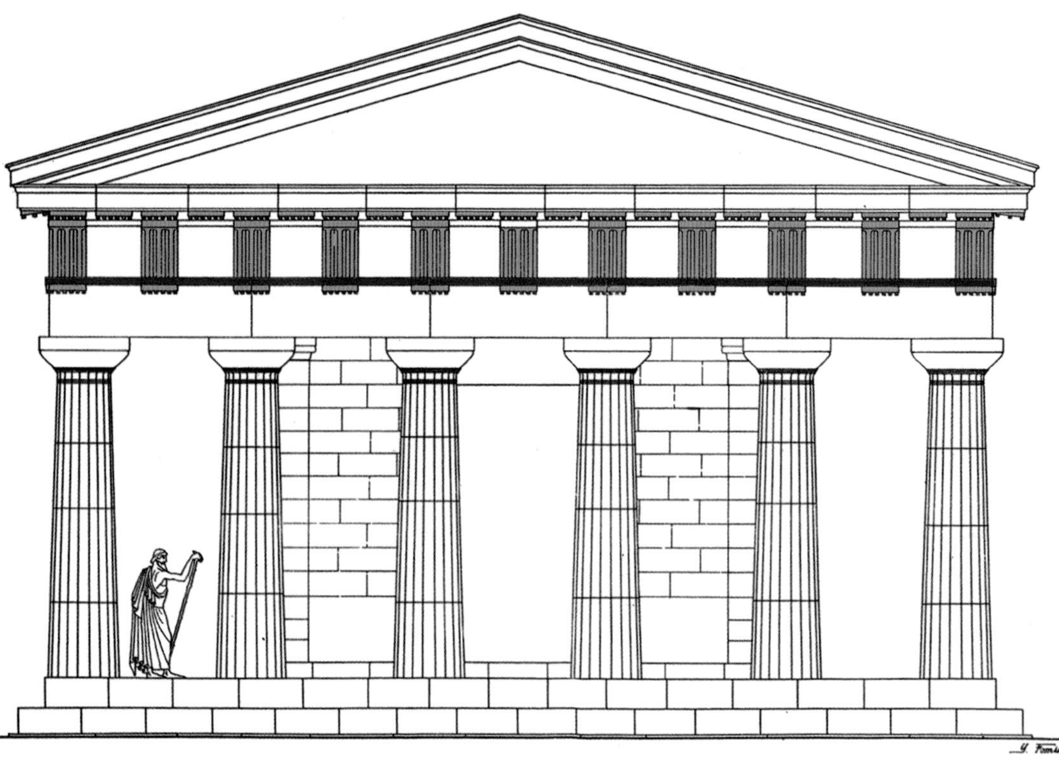

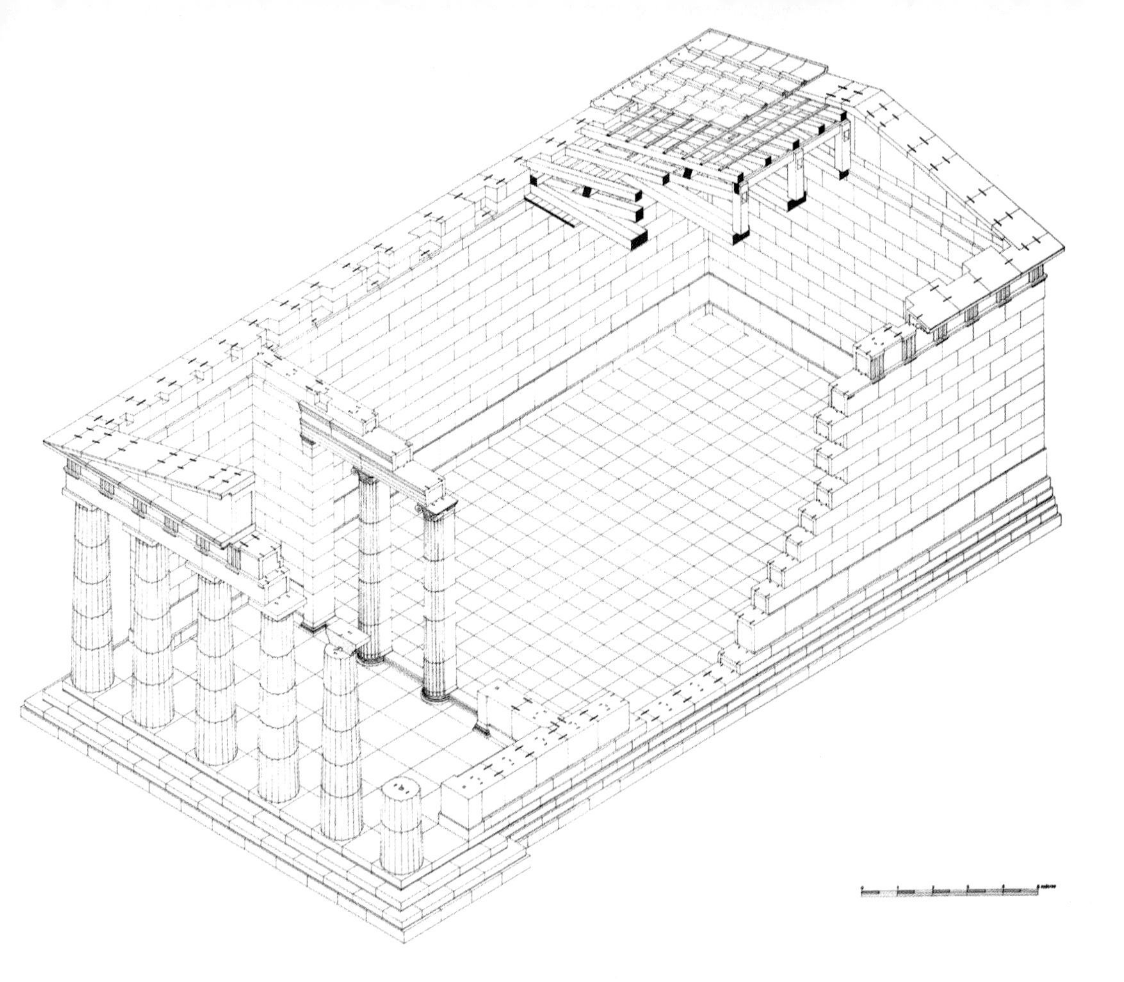

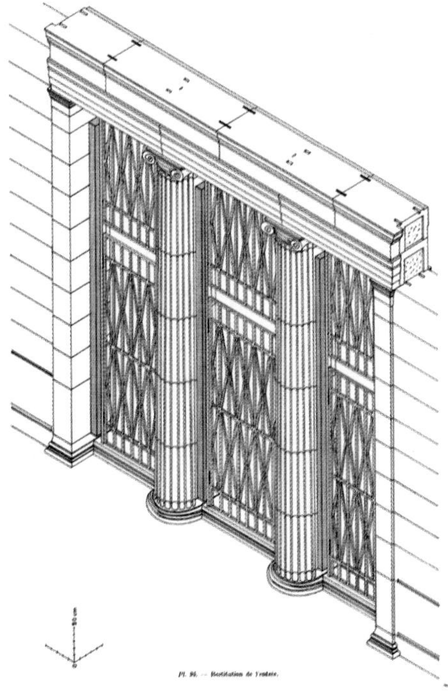

▲
▶ *Reconstruction and section of the triple opening into the cella of the later Temple of Athena Pronaia (F. D., J. P. Michaud).*

◀ *Reconstruction of the poros Temple of Athena Pronaia (Y. Fomine).*

outside frieze survive. This treasury was offered by the people of Marseille, who were Greek colonists from Phocaia, a city in Asia Minor. In the sekos a base for the statues of Roman emperors is still preserved.

Around the two treasuries are different bases with deep grooves for setting up inscribed stelai. An inscribed base from a statue of the emperor Hadrian was found by A. Keramopoullos, built into the south side of the enclosure wall. The large rectangular base **(9)** set obliquely to the two treasuries was perhaps for a trophy or other dedication from the Delphians, after the gods helped to drive back the Persians in 480 BC. Chr. Karouzos praises the arrangement of this monument: "The architectural picture of these monuments (as of others in the sanctuary) is not that of a lifeless row, but that of an animated group of statues, each with its own expression and movement". (Chr. Karouzos, *Delphi,* Athens 1974, p.65).

The circular Tholos **(6)** with its three restored columns dominates the ruins of Marmaria, as it must have in antiquity, because of its original circular appearance and the high standard of its decoration. It belongs to the decade 390-380 BC, a few years before the great earthquake, and its architect is thought to be Theodore from Phocaia in Asia Minor. He wrote a book on its excellence; he could be the same person as the architect Theodotos, who built the tholos at Epidauros a little later. The Tholos at Delphi has a diameter of 13.50 m and is built mostly of Pentelic marble on a crepis of three steps; twenty Doric columns outside supported the entablature and the lower roof of the circular colonnade. The metopes were decorated with sculptured reliefs of the Battles of the Amazons and

▲ *Reconstruction of the Tholos in the Sanctuary of Athena Pronaia (H. Pomtow).*

The Tholos in the Sanctuary of Athena Pronaia. ▶

the Centaurs. Another row of smaller metopes high on the outer wall of the colonnade portrayed the exploits of Theseus and the Labours of Heracles. The threshold of the entrance on the south side of the circular sekos is preserved, while the floor, of stone from Eleusis, is partly restored. Round the wall of the sekos inside are ten Corinthian half columns. The conical roof had marble tiles and akroteria. Parts of the architectural and sculptured decoration of the Tholos are on show in the Museum, but details, such as the Lesbian moulding running round the bottom of the wall and other mouldings, are still *in situ.*

The purpose of the Tholos is unknown and Pausanias, unfortunately, does not mention the wonderful building. It has been suggested that it was for the worship of a chthonic goddess, like the similar circular buildings at Epidauros, Olympia, the Athenian Agora, etc..

On the right of the Tholos, is a later temple to Athena Pronaia **(7)** built to replace the Archaic temple (3), which was destroyed in the earthquake of 373 BC. It is constructed of local limestone, from the quarries of Prophetes Elias, in the Doric order (22.60 by 11.55 m) with six Doric columns, on the facade only (a prostyle temple). It, too, has no opisthodomos, but it has a wider facade with two columns in the passage from the pronaos to the sekos; the metopes were undecorated. A base stood in the sekos in Roman times.

On the west side of the temple **(7)** lay an older building **(8)** 12.05 by 10.90 m. A prodomos running the width of the building gives entry to two rooms of about the same size, next to each other. Its polygonal walls date the building to the Archaic Period. Its purpose is uncertain but it is conventionally called the "House of the Priests". About 10 m to the west is the narrow west end of the enclosure wall of the Pronaia Sanctuary with an exit in the southwest corner to the nearby Gymnasium.

The Gymnasium

As is usual in Greece there is a myth attached to the Gymnasium: Odysseus was gored in the leg by a boar, while hunting here with the sons of Autolykos, and this old wound enabled his maid, Eurykleia, to recognise him when he returned to Ithaca. So here at the foot of Hyampeia, not far from the sacred Kastalian spring, the young men of Delphi trained on a track renowned because of a Homeric hero, the wily Odysseus. In mythical times this steep hillside must have been covered with thick undergrowth.

In ancient Greece the Gymnasium was used for many facets of education which are taught nowadays in schools, colleges, by military training, etc.. The area had to be landscaped to accomodate its many installations, such as race-tracks, terraces, stairs, a drainage and sewage system. The Gymnasium at Delphi lies on two terraces with the palaestra on the lower level and the xystos on the upper.

◀ *Restored part of the Tholos.*

The palaestra **(1)** is a building with a square peristyle inner court (the sides are 13.85 m long) with eight columns a side holding up the roof of a stoa. On the south and west sides are rooms of different dimensions, lay-out and purpose. The large room on the west side was probably the dressing room; on the north side one room was the konima or konisterion. Fine sand was kept here, which was used by the athletes with oil to anoint their bodies. Another room was a sphairisterion, where the boxers and pankratiasts trained with sandbags. The room on the west side, built on a temple plan with two columns at the entrance, an ante-chamber and a main room, possibly contained a statue of one or more of the gods connected with the Gymnasium (Hermes, Heracles) against the wall. This was perhaps the Ephebion or Exedra. In good weather training took place in the open court, in bad weather in the stoa. In later times the church of the Panayia **(2)** was built here and on one of its columns –in fact a Gymnasium column re-used– Lord Byron and his friend Hodhouse carved their names in 1809.

On the west side of the palaestra a bath with three steps is relatively well preserved **(3)**. On a retaining wall to the north are the remains, partly restored, of a marvellous fountain with eleven spouts and ten basins beneath them. The water came from Kastalia and drained into the circular bath. This was necessary in a Gymnasium so that the athletes could wash in cold water. A little futher west there were warm baths provided with a hypocaust **(4)**, which were constructed, along with two others in the Apollo Sanctuary, about 120 AD for the more demanding Romans.

On the upper terrace of the Gymnasium the *xystos* **(5)** can be seen, when the area is not overgrown. It is a huge colonnade running north-south and is longer than all the other palaestra buildings since it must have been about the

Plan of the Gymnasium: **1.** *Palaestra.* **2.** *Catholikon of the Monastery of the Assumption.* **3.** *Cistern.* **4.** *Bath.* **5.** *Covered running track.* **6.** *Open running track.*

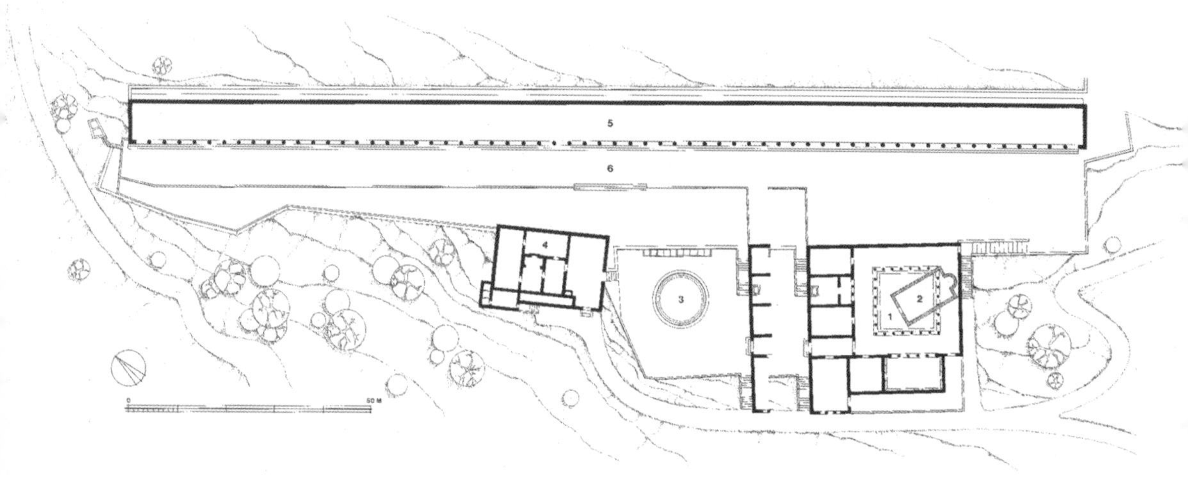

The Gymnasium.

length of a Delphic stade. The inner dimensions are 184.43 by 7.50 m. The colonnade was first constructed with poros columns in the Doric order but these were replaced in Roman times by marble Ionic ones on tall cubic bases. In order to be completely flat and solid the floor was scraped and thus the building was called a xystos (meaning scraped). The athletes trained here on the track on both wet and fine days. In good weather the *paradromis* was also used, a track outside and parallel to the stoa of the xystos **(6)**. During Hellenistic times and later the area of the Gymnasium was frequented by every type of teacher, poet, philosopher, orator, musician, etc.. In the festival of the Eumeneia a torch race began from the Gymnasium and ended in front of the Apollo Temple.

In the neighbourhood of the Gymnasium was an important sanctuary to Demeter. Pausanias does not mention it, perhaps because it was only separated from the Gymnasium by a small wall (teichion, as the inscriptions call it). It was located at the southeast end of the xystos by J. Jannoray, but in 1980 G. Roux, using inscriptions and other excavated material, placed it at the northwest end where, during excavation, small finds and other remains of cult were found in the rocks. He supposes that an ancient shrine to Demeter may have extended as far as the other side of the Kastalian stream.

The Spring of Kastalia

Above the Gymnasium is the Spring of Kastalia, of great importance to the site: Pindar rightly said that water was one of nature's best gifts. In antiquity the natural spring sufficed for a local cult, before man interfered; but the Greeks embellished even nature. There are two fountains. The archaic fountain was found by chance in 1959 when the road was broadened. It was partly restored in 1969 and 1977 and finally published by the former Director of the French School of Archaeology, Pierre Amandry (1977). It is a poros construction dating to the First Sacred War (600-590 BC). The water, rising at the base of Hyampeia, ran without pipes down to the fountain 50 m lower. About 460 BC a channel was constructed, partly cut in the rock, and covered with thick tiles. This channel was finally uncovered in 1977. The water collected in a built cistern with dimensions of about 6.5 by 1.5 m and fell from there through four lionshead spouts. The facade of the fountain was stuccoed and painted; traces of blue paint survive. The paved court in front (now partly restored) had benches around and a wall with high orthostates. Proceeding fifty metres towards the Cliff of Hyampeia cuttings can be seen in the rock, from which the water emerges, and, on the left, the narrow cleft between the Phaidriades. The water is always cold and good to taste, if drunk immediately from the spring. The second fountain was made in Hellenistic or Roman times, when the rock was cut and a small square levelled, in front of which were eight rock-cut steps. Beyond is the narrow rock-cut water cistern roughly one metre by half a metre. The water falls from the right and meets a sluice on the left which controls its

Below: Kastalian Fountain in the Archaic Period (A. K. Orlandos).
Opposite: Later Kastalian Spring.

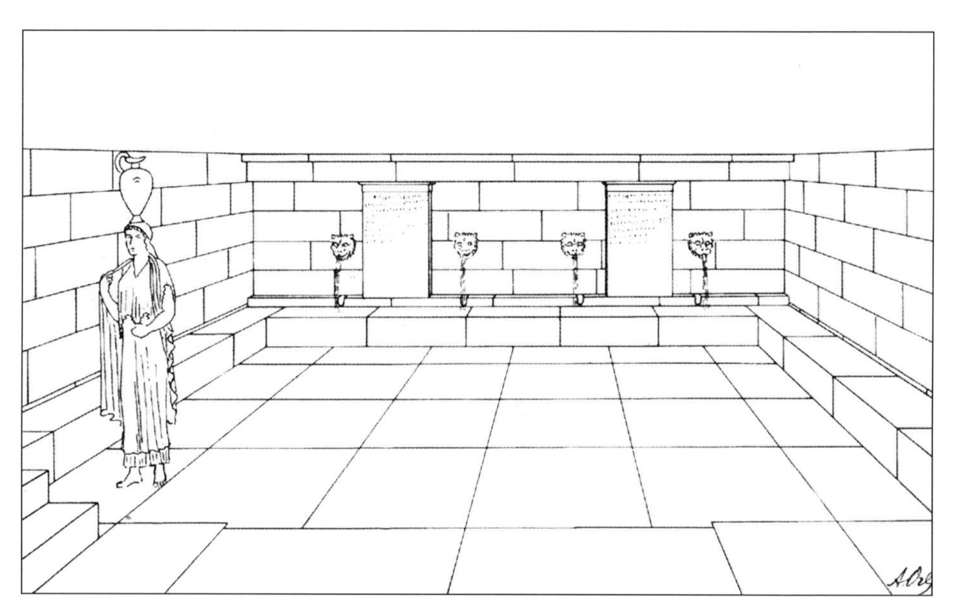

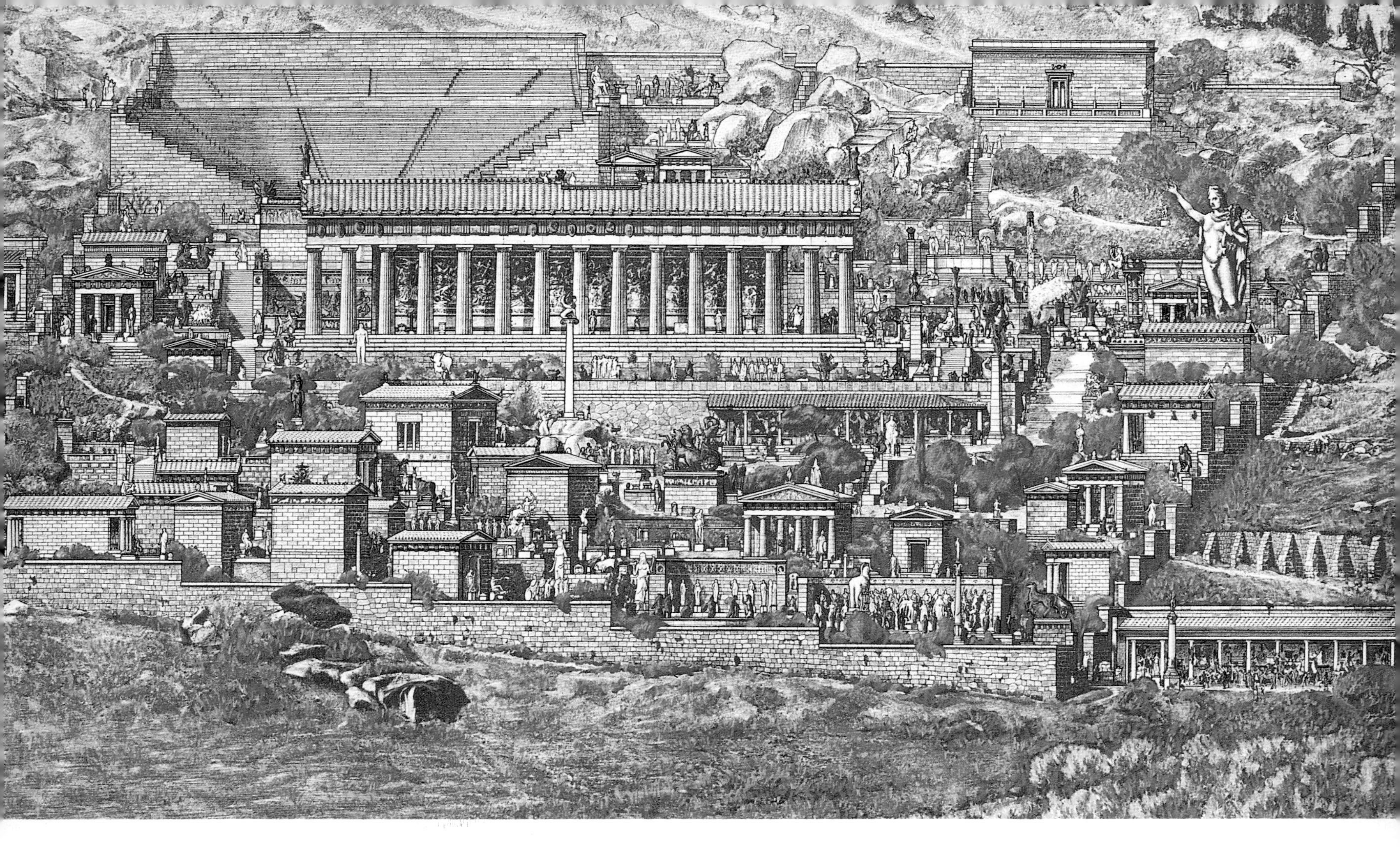

Reconstruction of the Sanctuary of Apollo, based on the plan of A. Tournaire (D. Svolopoulos).

level so that it flows through the seven spouts or so that the cistern can be emptied for cleaning. The spouts were probably decorated with lion or gorgon heads. The surrounding rock was covered with upright marble slabs to a height of 2.50 m. while higher up niches were cut in the cliff to receive offerings varying from figurines to biscuits. The small column drum in the large niche was used as an altar support in the later Christian shrine, where the worshippers lit their candles.

Although the architectural details of the fountains are mentioned here for today's archaeological visitors, they certainly did not interest the ancient worshippers who came to the sacred place with a religious awe, for not only the Pythia, but everyone else, including the priests, had to purify themselves here before entering the sanctuary or Apollo Temple to sacrifice, consult the oracle, or carry out any other religious ceremony. Near the archaic fountain to the east are the possible remains of the shrine to the hero Autonoos, mentioned with Phylacos above. He helped twice to save the sanctuary from foreign invasion, once from the Persians and once from the Galatians.

The Sanctuary of Apollo

In antiquity the town of Delphi and the higher Apollo Sanctuary covered almost the whole area visible from the Pronaia under the cliff of Rodini, ancient Nauplia. The appearance of this semi-circular place must have been fabulous when all the buildings were still standing surrounded by the "sacred wall of Apollo" as Pausanias called the sanctuary wall, which he describes after the Pronaia Temple and the Kastalian Spring.

This enclosure wall would be outstanding on its own for its craftsmanship, if it did not happen to contain so many other wonderful antiquities. It encompasses a steeply descending trapezoidal stretch (greatest dimensions 195 by 135 m) and was landscaped as early as the Archaic Period. It was repaired in the 5th and 4th centuries BC but its dimensions remained almost unchanged throughout its history, except for the 3rd century BC additions of the Stoa of the Aetolians to the west and the offerings of Attalos I in the east. The sanctuary was entered from the east (A, B, C, D) and west (A′, B′, C′, D′, E′) but the main entrance, which is used today, was in the southeast corner, where the Sacred Way begins.

The tiled square outside the main entrance is the Roman Agora **(1)** and betrays its Roman construction, especially on the north side where there were shops at the back of the Ionic stoa, in which suppliants and visitors could buy small offerings to Apollo, such as figurines, small vases and tripods, etc... Later on splendid processions were held here during the Pythian Games. Plinths and bases, some of which are preserved, supported statues of Roman emperors and other important people. The columns of the stoa have been restored (1977) and marble architectural fragments have been assembled in the stoa and shops together with Early Christian.

The level of the present day entrance to the sanctuary is a little higher than

THE SANCTUARY OF APOLLO

1. The Roman Agora
1a. Cercyraian Bull
2. Offering of the Arcadians
3. Spartan Monument
4. Base of offering
5. Athenian Offering
6. Dorian Horse
7. The Seven against Thebes, – The Epigoni
8. The Kings of Argos
9. Hellenistic Monument
10. Bronze Statue of Philopoemen
11-12. Two bases
13-14. Two niches
15. Tarentine Monument
16. Sicyonian Treasury
17. Statues from Cnidos
18. Aetolian Offering
19. Siphnian Treasury
20. Liparian Offering
21. Theban Treasury
22. Niche
23. Boeotian Treasury
24. Megarian Treasury
25. Syracusan Treasury
26. Treasury of Klazomenae
27. Treasury of Cnidos
28. Poteidaean Treasury
28a. The stone Omphalos
29. Unidentified archaic Treasury
30. The Treasury of Athenians
31. The Asclepieion
32. Archaic fountain
33. The Bouleuterion
34. Exedra of Herodes Atticus
35. The Spring of Ge
36. The rock of Sibyl
36a. The rock of Leto
37. Boeotian Offerings
37a. Doloneian Stair
37b. Halos
38. Exedrae
39. Monument with three columns
40. Unidentified archaic Treasury
41. The Naxian Sphinx
42. The Stoa of the Athenians
43. Corinthian Treasury
44. Treasury of Cyrene
45. The Prytaneion
46. Unidentified archaic Treasury
47. Treasury of Brasidas and the Acanthians
48. Tarantine Monument (second)
49. The Tripod of the citizens of Croton
49a. The Tripod of Plataea
50. The Chariot of Rhodes
51. «Oikos»
52. Offering of the Messenians
53. The Aemilius Paulus Monument
54. Stoa of Attalos I
55. The "oikos" of Attalos ("Dionysion")
56. Offerings of Attalos I
57. Statue of Attalos I
58. Statue of Eumenes II
59. Unidentified Treasury
60. Base of the statue of Eumenes II, offering of the Aetolians
60a. The Altar of Chios
61. Bronze palm tree
62. The monument of Aristaineta
63. The pedestal of the statue of Prousias
64. Apollo Sitalcas
65. The Tripods of the Deinomenids
66. Kassotis Spring
67. Statues of the Aitolian Generals
68. Cercyraian base
69. Horse-shoe shaped base
70. The Offering of Daochos II
71. Archaic polygonal wall
72. The Acanthus Column with dancing caryatids
73. Base of unidentified offering
74. "Temenos of Neoptolemos"
75. The Stone of Kronos
76. 4th century B.C. monument
77. The Cnidian Clubhouse
78. Supposed Messenian Offering
79. Temple of Apollo
80. Spring of the Muses
81-85. Unidentified archaic Treasuries
86-87. Statue bases
88. The Offering of Krateros
89-90. The great Stoa of the Aitolians
91. Unidentified Treasury
92. The Theatre
93-94. Unidentified Teasuries
95. The Poteidanion

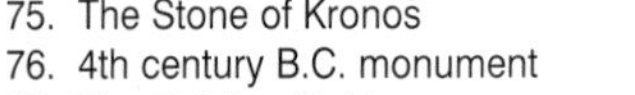

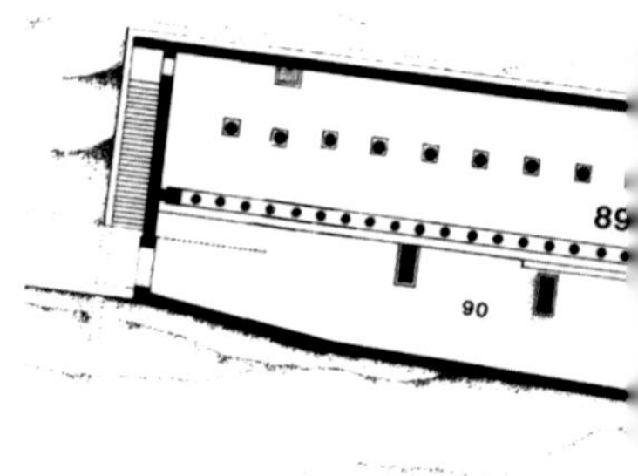

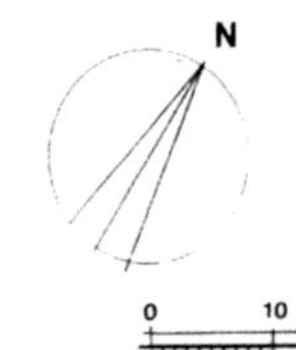

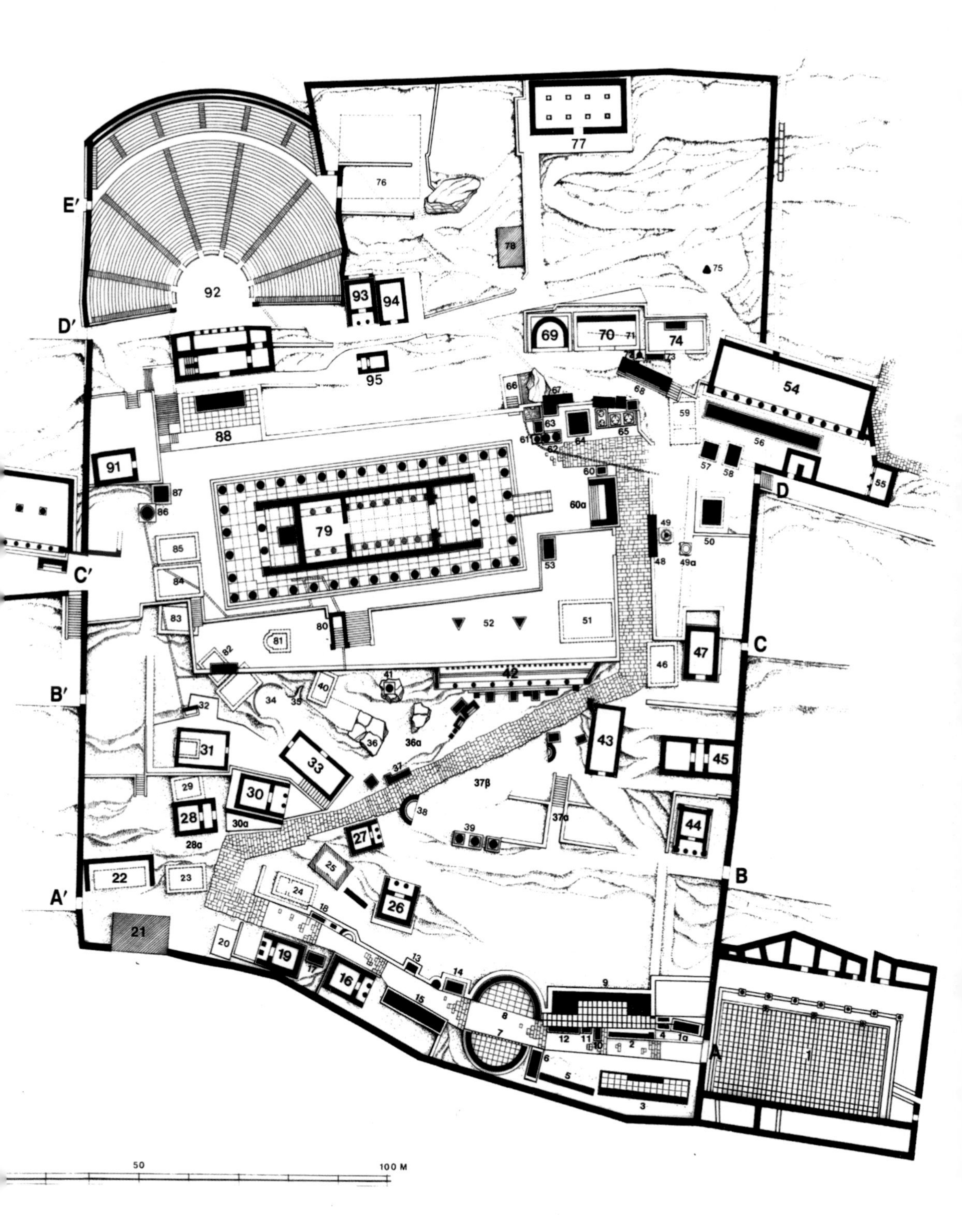

E′
D′
C′
B′
A′
A
B
C
D
50
100 M

the ancient one and the first part of the paving of the Sacred Way belongs to the years of decline.

On entering the sanctuary the visitor should remember its sanctity while enjoying its view. Moreover, he will find that at each change of position he will get a different picture of the monuments, whether he is looking at them as a group or at each one separately. Nowhere else have so many original works of art been assembled in their true surroundings and in such a small area. The whole sanctuary was full of votive offerings to delight the god (the ancient Greek word for statue was agalma, which literally meant an object of delight). Immediately past the entrance is the first stone base which belongs to the Cercyraian Bull (**1a**). Every offering has a myth or historical fact attached to it and that of the Cercyraian Bull will be told as an example. According to Pausanias (X. 9.3) a bull in Cercyra (Corfu) left his field, went down to the sea and bellowed on the shore. This occurred every day until finally the herdsman went to see what was wrong and saw a huge number of tunny fish in the sea. He went and told the inhabitants of Cercyra in the town and they tried in vain to catch the fish. Finally they sent to Delphi to ask what they should do and the

Below: Roman Agora. Opposite: General view of the Sanctuary of Apollo.

Pythia told them to sacrifice the bull to the god of the sea. As soon as they had carried out this sacrifice to Poseidon they were able to catch the fish, which they sold at a vast profit as there were so many, and, with a tenth of this, they offered a bronze bull at Olympia and another at Delphi. Pausanias probably heard this story from a contemporary guide. The base for the bull's statue is 4 by 5.20 m but it was originally taller than it is today and, together with the statue, it must have been very imposing. The bull was made in the decade 490-480 BC by the Aeginetan sculptor Theopropos, but, according to the inscription on its north side (above left), the base was made in the 4th century BC.

Further on an oblong base 9.40 m long supported the Offering of the Arcadians **(2)**. Its inscription corrects Pausanias, who notes that it was an offering from the Arcadian city of Tegea only. Above this base stood a line of nine bronze statues: Apollo, Nike (Victory), Callisto (mythical mother of the eponymous hero, Arcas), Arcas (founder of the Arcadians) and his children, Elatos, Areidas, Azan, Triphylos and Erasos. The offering was made after the Arcadians attacked Laconia with their ally the Theban general Epaminondas in 369 BC.

On the left opposite the Arcadian offering was the Spartan Monument **(3)** consisting, according to Pausanias, of 38 bronze statues by different craftsmen. Among others Lysander was depicted being crowned by Poseidon, the Dioscuri, Zeus, Apollo, Artemis and the Spartan generals and admirals who, under Lysander, defeated the Athenians at the great naval battle of Aegospotami in 404 BC, the final year of the Peloponnesian War. Pausanias gives their names. This monument of "the admirals" was set up after the defeat

◀ *Reconstruction of the Cercyraian Bull (H. Pomtow).*

Temenos of Apollo: the Phaidriades with the river Pleistos in the background. In the centre, below the road: the Gymnasium and Sanctuary of Athena Pronaia. ▶

of the Athenians next to their already existing monument (below no. 5).

The Argives offered the Trojan Horse **(6)** made of bronze. It was made by the Argive sculptor, Antiphanes, as an offering to Apollo from the spoils of their victory over the Spartans at the Battle of Thyreatis 414 BC.

The Athenian Offering **(5)** already mentioned, which is earlier than that of the Peloponnesians and later only than the Cercyraian Bull, is the first of a series of Athenian offerings which line the Sacred Way. It depicts Miltiades, the victor of the Battle of Marathon, with the deities of Delphi and Athens, ie. Apollo and Athena, and the seven eponymous heroes of the Attic tribes. The offering was not made immediately after Marathon, but after his honours had been restored to Miltiades, perhaps by his son Cimon, about 460 BC. Much later the three eponymous kings of the new tribes, Antigonos of Macedon, his son, Demetrius Polyorketes and another Macedonian king, Ptolemy of Egypt, were added to the seven eponymous heroes of the Attic tribes. West of the offering of the Athenians and the Dorian Horse of the Argives was another offering of

the Argives: in the semi-circular space with a diameter of 12 m were depicted the Seven Against Thebes **(7)**, the seven mythical leaders of the Argives, when they were making war against Eteocles, with Amphiaraus on his chariot driven by the charioteer Baton. The bronze statues of the Epigoni, their sons, who unlike their unfortunate fathers captured and destroyed Thebes, were probably placed in the same place. The statues were the works of the sculptors Hypatodorus and Aristogeiton.

The short inscription cut in large letters tells us simply that "Argives erected these to Apollo", but the traveller Pausanias writes that the monument was put up after the victory of the allies of the Athenians and Argives over the Spartans at Oinoë (west of Argos) in 456 BC.

Opposite the semi-circle of the Epigoni was another semi-circular Argive offering, the kings of Argos **(8)**, consisting of ten bronze statues of heroes and mythical kings of Argos. First came Danaos with his daughter Hypermnestra, and other members of the family, ending with Alcmene and Heracles. The myth in which Alcmene gave birth to Heracles in Thebes united Argos and Thebes. This offering was meant to commemorate the link, but was made when the Argives needed Theban friendship after 370 BC. The monument, made by the Argive sculptor, Antiphanes, was set up after the foundation of the city of Messene in 369 BC, by the Argives and the Theban general, Epaminondas. Behind the monuments on the right side of the Sacred Way already described are the ruins of a Hellenistic Monument **(9)** with a rectangular niche. Nothing is known about this monument and, as it is almost invisible, it need not detain the visitor.

In front of this anonymous monument is the rectangular base of the bronze Statue of Philopoemen **(10)**, a general of the Achaian League. The inscription reads that the Achaians set up the monument because Philopoemen was valiant and considerate. On the other hand, Plutarch writes that Philopoemen was depicted killing Machanidas, the Spartan tyrant, after the Battle of Mantineia 207 BC.

The following two bases **(11-12)** and the two niches **(13-14)** beyond the Argive offering (8) have not been identified and make a good point for the visitor to look back on the first ten offerings on the Sacred Way, which must have contained over a hundred bronze statues of gods, demi-gods, mythical representations and historical personalities, generals, admirals, a bull, the Trojan Horse, groups of equestrian fighters and, probably, many other small offerings which have disappeared. They must have presented a wonderful picture of Greek mythology, religion, history and art.

Continuing up the Sacred Way part of the base of the Tarentine Monument **(15)** is preserved on the left together with part of the offering inscription. Taras was a Spartan colony in south Italy (Magna Graecia). After their victory against the Messapi at the beginning of the 5th century BC the Tarentines set up this monument from a tenth of the spoil. It depicted female prisoners and horses and was made by the famous Argive bronze sculptor, Ageladas.

The scenery changes with the ruins of the first Treasury, the Sicyonian Treasury **(16)**. In antiquity the east side of this treasury, which is built on a temple plan with two columns *in antis,* would have been seen from the Sacred Way. Today only the ruins of its poros foundations remain, which re-use the

Reconstruction of the Treasury of the Siphnians (A. Tournaire).

poros circular and rectangular blocks from two earlier treasuries. The two older treasuries on the same site consisted of a tholos, with a diameter of 6.32 m and thirteen Doric columns round it, and a monopteros – a building with a roof supported by columns, but no sekos. It was about 4.20 by 5.50 m and had 4 by 5 Doric columns. The metopes on show in the Museum belong to this building. According to one version, the chariot, in which Cleisthenes, Tyrant of Sicyon, won the Pythian Games in 582 BC, was displayed in the monopteros. At about this time the circular treasury (the tholos) was set up. The later Sicyonian Treasury was built in 500 BC by the oligarchs who had pushed the Orthagorid tyrants out of Sicyon.

It is thought that statues from Cnidos **(17)** in Asia Minor stood between the Sicyonian and the following Siphnian Treasury (19), while opposite them, on the other side of the Sacred Way, was an Aetolian Offering **(18)**.

The Siphnian Treasury **(19)** was one of the most beautiful buildings at Delphi. This small Aegean island reached its acme in the mid-6th century BC gathering wealth from its gold and silver mines. About 525 BC refugees from Samos, who had revolted against the tyranny of Polykrates and plundered the island, so it is thought that the treasury must have been constructed before this time. A part from the foundations, it is built, side by side with the Sicyonian Treasury, of beautiful Parian marble on the usual treasury plan of a megaron, facing west. At this point a small square, like a stair landing, is made by the Sacred Way turning a corner, while another flatter road comes from the south gate of the temple (A'). In antiquity the visitor to this Ionic treasury would first have admired the two female statues (caryatids), who supported the entablature and the pediment, and the carved frieze round the four sides of the building whose total length was 29.63 m. The preserved parts of the caryatid, frieze sculpture and pediment are on show in the Museum.

Following the road towards the exit (A'), on the left is the Liparian Offering base **(20)**. They inhabited the largest of the Aeolian Islands, north of Sicily. Further on are the ruins of the beautiful Theban Treasury **(21)**, built after the Battle of Leuctra 371 BC with inscriptions of honour cut in its walls. Opposite is a worn base **(22)** in a rectangular niche and the remains of another older Boeotian Treasury **(23)** with names carved on the foundation stones.

Returning to the "stair landing" the Megarian Treasury **(24)** can be identified from the decrees of the city of Megara, which are carved on the restored wall in front of the treasury. It used to be thought that this treasury belonged to the Syracusans but now a nearby one (25) is attributed to them. It was built after their victory over the Athenians in 413 BC opposite that of the Athenians. However, few traces of the Megarian Treasury remain, while a corner triglyph of black stone with a white marble cornice of the Doric Syracusan Treasury has been preserved.

Near the Syracusan Treasury **(25)** were two treasuries belonging to cities in Asia Minor. That in the Aeolic order was perhaps the Treasury of Klazomenae **(26)** while near it is the Treasury of Cnidos **(27)** built in the Ionic order with fine architectural decoration in 550-545 BC with a tenth of the booty from some victory. This could have been the prototype of the Siphnian Treasury, as it also had caryatids.

Near the place where a stone omphalos **(28a)** has been set up from elsewhere is the supposed Poteidaean Treasury **(28)** belonging to a town in the Chalcidic Peninsular; it was built of poros about 500 BC. There are the few

Treasury of the Athenians.

Reconstruction of the SE corner of the facade of the Treasury of the Athenians (A. Tournaire).

Reconstruction of the facade of the Treasury of the Athenians (A. Tournaire).

remains of another unidentified Archaic treasury **(29)** close by. The Treasury of the Athenians **(30)** is one of the most famous offerings and, since its restoration, is perhaps the hallmark of the sanctuary at Delphi. It was worked on and restored (1903-06) by the French architect, Replat, at a cost of 35.000 gold drachmae, payed for by the city of Athens. It is built of Parian marble in the Doric order on the usual temple plan with columns *in antis.* It is 9.687 m long and 6.621 m wide. It had 30 sculptured metopes: the six on the facade show the Amazonomachy, the nine on the south side show the Labours of the Athenian hero, Theseus, the nine on the north side the Labours of Heracles, as also the six on the west side, where the theft of the cattle of Geryon is depicted. The 24 best preserved metopes are on show in the Museum and their gypsum replicas are in the restored building. The pediments above were also decorated with sculptured reliefs (Theseus and Perithous on the east and a battle scene on the west). There is some doubt whether the treasury was built before or (according to Pausanias) after the Battle of Marathon, but it is certain that Persian arms from this Athenian victory were displayed on a triangular base **(30a)** running along the south side on the outside, as a large inscription on the base relates.

On the other hand, from the third century BC and onwards, inscriptions began to be cut on the walls, especially decrees honouring Athenian citizens. The inscriptions on the south wall are particularly interesting; carved between 138 and 128 BC, they consist of two hymns to Apollo with the ancient notes for voices and musical instruments. They are now in the Museum.

Behind the Athenian Treasury at a lower level the ruins of a small unidentified Archaic temple can be distinguished between the better preserved and partly restored ruins of the Asclepieion **(31)**. A little to the north an Archaic fountain **(32)**, the Spring of the Asclepieion, is fairly well preserved (somewhat restored in 1977). Next to the Athenian Treasury are the ruins of a relatively long, oblong, poros building, the Bouleuterion **(33)**, recently partly restored. The fifteen councillors of the city of Delphi met here and made decisions.

Above the Bouleuterion, a little to the west, are the scarcely visible ruins of an unidentified Archaic treasury, but the exedra can be seen, which is assumed to be the offering of Herodes Atticus **(34)**.

Nearby are some of the oldest and most holy ruins at Delphi. The Spring of Ge **(35)**, owner of the sanctuary before Apollo, was guarded by the Pytho, whom Apollo killed. Themis, goddess of justice, and Poseidon, initially god of the freshwater underground streams, were also worshipped here. Nearby is the Rock of the Sibyl **(36)**, known from Plutarch and Pausanias, which must have fallen from the Phaidriades thousands of years ago. In antiquity it was believed the first Sibyl began to give oracles from here, when she came from Troy. Above the Sybilline Rock, to the north, a smaller rock is the so-called rock of Leto **(36a)**, as, according to the myth, Leto stood here holding the infant Apollo while he shot the Pytho. This is depicted on the clay akroteria of the temple of the Etruscan city of Veii in modern Lazio. The area surrounding these antiquities was destroyed when the Apollo Temple and its retaining wall were constructed after 548 BC.

Section of the Sacred Way. Right: Treasury of the Athenians and Rock of the Sybil.

In front of the Rocks of Sibyl and Leto is a line of different bases from Boeotian offerings **(37)**. Opposite them on the other side of the Sacred Way, at an equal distance from the Bouleuterion (33) and the Prytaneion (45), lies the *Halos* **(37b)** a place kept free of buildings for the Septeria, a religious drama which was held every eight years. A portrayal of Apollo's killing of the Pytho took place: a child with both parents living, played the role of Apollo and members of the family of the Labyades took him up the Doloneian Stair **(37a)** with lighted torches the child pointed to the serpent's nest and the torchbearers set it on fire. Then everyone left without looking back, as Apollo did when he fled to Tempe to be purified.

By this part of the Halos the chryselephantine objects, the silver bull and other finds were found under the paving of the Sacred Way in two pits in 1939. They are on show in the Museum. Different monuments surround the area of the Halos, such as exedrae **(38)** and a monument with three columns **(39)**, etc.

On the left of the Sacred Way are the ruins of an unidentified archaic treasure **(40)** and the base of the famous Naxian Sphinx **(41)** on show in the Museum. Only many scattered pieces from the drums, with characteristic shallow grooves, of the column, on which the Sphinx stood, remain on the spot. It was more than 12 m high.

On the same level looking towards the ascending Sacred Way is the long Stoa of the Athenians **(42)** with many bases down the length of the facade for the different offerings, including one Boeotian offering. The Stoa was constructed after 478 BC to house the spoils from the naval victories of the Athenians over the Persians. It was built in the Ionic order against the polygonal retaining wall for the embankment of the Apollo temple and was 30 m long, but only 4 m deep. On the facade between the pilasters stood eight thin fluted marble columns, each made from a single stone, which supported the wooden roof. On the stylobate the large lettered inscription, which is still legible, relates that the Athenians offered: a) the Stoa, b) the flax cables which held together the bridge of boats by which Xerxes' army crossed the Hellespont and c) the prows with bronze figureheads from the Persian ships. The polygonal retaining wall with its curving joints mentioned above is in itself a work of art and a monument to the knowledge of the ancient world. About eight hundred inscriptions are carved on it, most of them acts of manumission.

Opposite the east end of the Stoa of the Athenians on the right side of the Sacred Way are the few remains of the oblong Corinthian Treasury **(43)** built near the Doloneian Stair. They are important as this treasury, which was perhaps built in the 7th century BC, is the oldest of the Delphic treasuries. Further east, at a lower level, near Gate B, is the possible Treasury of Cyrene **(44)** built in the Doric order on the usual plan with two columns *in antis.* To the north of this and on a higher terrace held by a retaining wall is the Prytaneion (Magistrates Hall) **(45)** built against the enclosure wall. It has an odd plan with two symmetrical rooms right and left of a corridor with an entrance to the north. Higher up the hill supported by another retaining wall are the ruins of an unidentified archaic treasury **(46)** and, next to it, the Treasury of Brasidas and the Acanthians **(47)** built after their victory against the Athenians at Amphipolis.

Ascending the Sacred Way, on the left is the end of the Polygonal Retaining wall with its many inscriptions, and on the right are the ruins of at least four buildings, one behind the other. The first is the second Tarantine Monument **(48)** (see above **(15)** for the first one), and behind it is a circular base **(49)**. This is thought nowadays to have been the base for a Tripod dedicated by the citizens of Croton at Delphi after their victory against Sybaris. A little further on is the probable base of the famous gold Tripod of Plataia **(49a)**, a votive offering for the victory at Plataia (479 BC). The Phocaians stole the gold Tripod during the Third Sacred War (356-346 BC). The column formed by three bronze serpents twined together, on which the gold cauldron was mounted, was carried off by Constantine the Great to Constantinople and still stands in the Hippodrome there today, engraved with the names of the cities that took part in the victorious battle against the Persians. The large base of the monument of the Rhodians **(50)** is also still in its place and stands out conspicuously, belonging to the gilded Chariot of Rhodes, dedicated in 304 BC.

Opposite the Monument of the Tarantines (48) an opening in the polygonal wall leads to the embankment south of the Apollo Temple. There, lower down,

Below: Stone paved Sacred Way. On the left, part of an Ionic column with capital and right, Stoa of the Athenians. Opposite: Stoa of the Athenians.

are the ruins of another unidentified archaic treasury **(51)** and the supposed position of the double offering of the Messenians in Naupactos **(52)**, two statues on triangular bases of Nike, like the Nike of Paionios at Olympia. Leaving the west part of the embankment for later, the Aemilius Paulus Monument **(53)** can be seen. It was being prepared as an offering by Perseus, the last king of Macedon, when this Roman general conquered him at the Battle of Pydna 168 BC. This battle not only brought about the end of Macedonian rule, but also involved the yielding of all Greece to the Romans. Thus, the victorious Aemilius Paulus set up his 12 m high equestrian statue on the base of his defeated opponent. This base with its sculptures of the Battle of Pydna is preserved and is now exhibited in the Museum. Returning to the Sacred Way, and omitting for the moment the Altar of Chios (60a) on the left, on the right were a number of monuments dedicated by the Attalids of Pergamon, accessible in antiquity also from the north Gates (D′, E′) in the enclosure wall. The large twostoried Stoa of Attalos **(54)**, who died in 197 BC, was changed into a reservoir in the 4th century AD for the baths outside the sanctuary. The "House of Attalos" **(55)** is supposed to be the "Dionysion". A

Stoa of the Athenians. Detail.

magnificent base for the Offerings of Attalos I **(56)** and two statue bases of Attalos I **(57)** and Eumenes II **(58)**, who died in 159 BC, put up by the Amphictyonic League, complete the Attalid monuments. A few ruins from one more unidentified treasury **(59)** are preserved west of the Attalid offerings. Returning to the square in front of the Apollo Temple the Altar of Chios **(60a)** lies on the left. This large altar, 8.60 by 5.10 m, was dedicated to Apollo in the 5th century BC, according to Herodotus and the inscription on it. For this the right of promanteia was given to the Chians (inscribed in the southeast corner). It was made from black marble, apart from the base and epistepsis, which were of white marble. Steps from the side of the temple lead up to it. It was repaired in the 3rd and 1st centuries BC and is now partly restored. On the north side of the altar is the base of the statue of the king of Pergamum, Eumenes II **(60)**. It was a votive offering of the *koinon* of the Aetolians, dated between 197-182 BC.

The north side of the square in front of the temple is crowded with monuments of different dates because of its important situation. From west to east are: the base for a bronze palm tree **(61)**, which supported a gold-plated statue of Athena, an Athenian offering made after their victory over the Persians

Part of the polygonal retaining wall with visible inscriptions.

Reconstruction of the Tripod of the Plataeans and the Acanthus Column of the Dancers (D. Laroche).

Reconstruction of the statue base for Aemilius Paulus (A. Tournaire).

on the River Eurymedon; the bicolumnar monument of the lady Aristaineta **(62)**; the high base for the statue of Prousias of Bithynia **(63)** dedicated, according to its inscription, by the Aetolian Confederacy; the very large base of the statue of Apollo Sitalcas **(64)** which was 16 m high, dedicated by the Amphictyonic League from the fine the Phocians paid. The epithet Sitalcas signifies Apollo's role as protector of grain so that the harvests should be good.

Three bases further east were for the gold Tripods of the Deinomenids **(65)**, Hiero, Polyzalos and Thrasyboulos, tyrants of Gela and Syracuse in Sicily. They were the sons of Deinomenes, Tyrant of Syracuse. The tripods were dedicated after the victory over the Carthaginians at Himera in 480 BC. The Phocians carried them off during the Third Sacred War. In the Museum is part of another offering made by Polyzalos, the famous bronze charioteer.

The Spring Kassotis, like the Kastalian Spring, played an important role in the ceremonial side of the cult, especially that on the oracle. In contrast to Kastalia, Kassotis **(66)** was only recently located behind the base of Prousias. It was believed that the waters plunged into the earth and flowed up again in

The end of the Sacred Way in front of the Temple of Apollo.

the temple. The spring took its name from a nymph of Parnassos. Higher up behind the Deinomenid offerings are the statue bases of the Aetolian Generals **(67)** and another so-called Cercyraion base **(68)**.

Further uphill is a row of important dedications which are now easily accessible as the area has been cleared. First is a horse-shoe shaped base **(69)**, which supported at least seventeen Hellenistic marble statues. To the east is an oblong base belonging to the Offering of Daochos II **(70)**, the Thessalian tetrarch, who was a hieromnemon of the Delphian Amphictyonic League (336-332 BC) and a friend of Philip II of Macedon. The inscribed bases of nine statues are preserved, belonging to Apollo, the donor, his ancestors and his son. The offering has been put together in the Museum by P. Themelis. There are traces of an archaic polygonal wall **(71)** by the Daochos offering.

The Acanthus Column **(72)**, an offering on a poros base with the letters PAN (krates), a well-known contractor from Delphi, is peculiar. It was 10.90 m high and supported a tripod with a bronze bowl, which was also supported on

Base of the statue of Prousias. ▶

◀ *The square in front of the Temple of Apollo and the restored ramp to the pronaos.*

the heads of three caryatids dancing between the tripod feet. Recent study has shown that the Omphalos also belonged to this monument. It was constructed about 350-320 BC and was probably an Athenian dedication. The dancers and column drums are on show in the Museum. The rectangular base of another unidentified offering **(73)** is attached to the above.

Behind these bases is a spacious building known as the "Temenos of Neoptolemos" **(74)**. Neoptolemos was the son of the Homeric hero Achilles who, according to legend, was killed by a priest of Apollo at Delphi and buried here. Higher up is roughly the place where the Stone of Kronos **(75)** was thought to have lain. This stone, which was not very big, according to Pausanias, received a daily libation of oil and other things, as it was believed to have been coughed up by Kronos, who had swallowed it instead of his son Zeus.

There high up, east of the Theatre, the curious visitor may look for and discover still more noteworthy monuments. Near the upper row of the Theatre **(76)** are the ruins of a 4th century BC monument which was not finished. Higher still, attached to the north wall of the enclosure, are the remains of the famous Cnidian Clubhouse **(77)**. A terrace was made to receive the rectangular hall 18.70 by 9.53 m, whose roof was supported by two rows of four wooden posts. It was entered from the south side and had a bench all round the walls. It owed its fame to the paintings by the famous Thasian artist, Polygnotos, which covered the walls. They were painted in the mid-5th century when the club was built. On the right of the entrance the Fall of Troy was depicted and on the left the Descent of Odysseus to Hades. These paintings were copied in vase painting and other art, and extant vases are examined to see if they bear a likeness to the work of Polygnotos, which is extensively described by Pausanias (X. 25.31). An inscription relates, however, that the paintings were touched up by three painters sent by Attalos I.

Descending from the Cnidian Clubhouse to the Apollo Temple, among retaining walls, are the remains of a base of a supposed Messenian Offering **(78)**.

This description of the monuments of the northeast corner digresses from the usual visitor's route but is necessary for a complete tour of the sanctuary. Returning now to the square in front of the Apollo Temple **(79)**, the visitor can see the remains of the building which must once have dominated the sanctuary. It has undergone centuries of successive catastrophes and rebuilding, but ancient authors and archaeological finds allow a fairly good reconstruction of its different appearances and the phases of its cult.

The last rebuilding occurred in the 4th century BC, but legend recounts that the first temple was a simple hut of laurel leaves from the Vale of Tempe. The second mythical temple was also made from material which came from the north: wax and feathers (ptera, hence the name Pterinos Naos) sent by Apollo from the Hyperboreans. The third temple was of bronze. The fourth and first historical temple was of poros and was built, with Apollo's help, by the mythical

Temple of Apollo from NW. ▶

architects, Trophonios and Agamedes, according to a Homeric Hymn to Pythian Apollo. Excavated traces of it belong to the 7th century BC. Its architectural fragments have been found built into the back part of the polygonal retaining wall, at the spring **(80)**, which was probably dedicated to the Nymphs, between this wall and the temple, and elsewhere. This temple was burnt in 548 BC and was shortly rebuilt. The new building was the so-called archaic temple or Alcmaeonid Temple, named after the noble Athenian family. The cost was met by gifts from the whole Greek world (and Amasis of Egypt) and from the contributions of the Amphictyonic League. The Alcmaeonids, who had been exiled by Peisistratos, were the contractors for the construction and paid more than their allotted share to construct the facade and the reliefs of the east pediment from Parian marble instead of poros (see below in the Museum). This temple was destroyed by an earthquake in 373 BC. Its reconstruction was delayed by the Third Sacred War (356-346 BC), but with the help of all Greece it was again rebuilt on the plan, and with almost the same dimensions, as the Alcmaeonid Temple, with six columns at the ends and fifteen down each side, that is with archaic proportions. It was finished about 330 BC. Poros was used for the columns and entablature, while the rest was of black marble from Parnassos. The first architect was Spintharos of Corinth, then, after his death, his co-citizens, Xenodoros and Agathon. The reliefs were made by the Athenian artists, Praxias and Androsthenes (see below in the Museum).

Reconstruction of the Temple of the Alcmaeonids and Stoa of the Athenians (P. Amandry).

Reconstruction of the facade of the Temple of the Alcmaeonids (H. Lacoste).

The present ruins belong to the 4th century BC temple. The foundations were of stone from the quarries of Prophetes Elias to the west of Delphi; the poros columns, six of which are now partly restored using the ancient material, were plastered; the temple was entered by a ramp, which was customary in Peloponnesian Temples. The partly preserved tiled floor of the pteron, pronaos and opisthodomos give an idea of the plan of the interior, as the walls have been robbed out for the lead of the clamps in their stones. On the north side an attempt at the restoration of the sekos has taken place and a column drum from the colonnade of the pteron has been put on the stylobate, on the three steps which form the crepis. The roof and pedimental reliefs were of Parian marble. According to Pausanias, the arrival of Apollo at Delphi was depicted on the east pediment, as also on that of the Alcmaeonid Temple, while on the west pediment Dionysos was portrayed with the Maenads (Thyiads). The metopes carried no sculptures but Persian shields were added to them after Marathon and Galatian after 279 BC. The Alcmaeonid sculptures, the omphalos, adyton, etc. are described below in the Museum section. The walls of the pronaos carried inscriptions on herms with the sayings of the seven sages of Greece such as "Know thyself" and "Nothing to Excess". The letter "E" was also inscribed and, when Plutarch was a priest at Delphi, he wrote a whole treatise on this, without making clear what it meant. There was also a bronze statue of Homer with the words of an oracle given to the blind poet on its base. The sekos was divided in two: in front was an altar to Poseidon, the forerunner of Apollo, statues of two Fates of Zeus Moiragetes and Apollo Moiragetes. There was also an iron throne, on which Pindar sat, when he came to Delphi and sang hymns to Apollo. The altar of Hestia in the pronaos was regarded as an altar for all the Greeks, it was here that the priests of Apollo killed Neoptolemos, the son of Achilles (see no. 74 above). The inner part of the sekos, the adyton, has been described above with the oracle and methods of prophesy. Pausanias says that very few had the right of entry to the adyton where, among other things, the gold statue of Apollo was placed. Kassotis, the prophetic fountain of Ge and the Muses, which had been incorporated into the temple in the archaic period, was moved, perhaps for safety, outside the temple to the north (see no. 66 above).

High above the temple, in the west part of the sanctuary are the spring of the older Kassotis (Kassotis I), the Spring of the Muses **(80)** and the remains of two unidentified archaic treasuries **(81-82)** with three more **(83-85)** lower down. North of the temple is the long retaining wall, the *Ischegaon* (ischo = to retain, ga = earth). Its name is mentioned in the inscriptions of the accounts for the rebuilding of the temple in the 4th century BC (after 356 BC). The bronze

Crepis of the Temple of Apollo.

charioteer was found crushed by falling rocks behind the Ischegaon. A statue of some sort probably stood in a niche in the Ischegaon (marked on the plan).

Northwest of the temple going towards the theatre there are statue bases **(86-87)** on the left while to the right the famous Offering of Krateros **(88)** is set in a rectangular niche. A well-known scene from Alexander's march into Asia was shown here. According to the description of Plutarch, the general Krateros saved Alexander's life at a lionhunt near Susa in Persia. The general's son, also called Krateros, dedicated the offering after 320 BC. The bronze group was made by the great sculptors of the epoch, Lysippus and Leochares. The inscription, high on the wall of the niche, narrates this story, which was illustrated many times, the most famous example being that found in 1957 at Pella in Macedonia.

Through the nearby Gate C′ in the enclosure wall is the great Stoa of the Aetolians **(89-90)**, identified by an inscription on the inner wall. It was built from the proceeds of booty taken at the victory of 279 BC over the Galatians. A colonnade on the facade supported the stoa roof and another further inside divided the building in two. In Roman times the east section of the stoa was adapted for baths. In front of the stoa are offering bases.

Restored columns of the Temple of Apollo.

A magnificent stair leads to the theatre from the Krateros Offering. It was possibly never completed because, as it is now, it is a blind alley and the present ascent is by a road almost parallel to the ancient stair. The remains of an unidentified treasury **(91)** lie by this road.

The Theatre **(92)** has all the usual appointments of an ancient Greek theatre and is one of the better preserved. It was originally built in the 4th century BC of white stone from Parnassos and probably replaced an earlier one made of wood. The auditorium has 35 rows of seats divided by a gangway which was accessible from Gate E΄ in the enclosure wall, the lower part and stage being reached by Gate D΄. Eight stairways facilitated circulation in the lower part of the auditorium and divided it into seven tiers. The narrowness of the area above the gangway limits the tiers there to six, although a full semi-circle should have had double those below, ie. fourteen. The theatre was enlarged in the 2nd century BC with money and slaves sent by Eumenes II of Pergamon about 159 BC, according to an inscription. In the 1st century AD a marble frieze was added to the metopes of the skene (stage-building) representing the Labours of Heracles. It is on show in the Museum. The skene was in two parts with a proskenium in front divided in three parts corresponding to those in the building behind it. The skene was low so that the audience could enjoy the wonderful view. The orchestra, 18.50 m in diameter, was tiled and had a gutter for drainage all round it. The seating capacity is about 5000. At the big festivals the emphasis was on dramatic and lyrical performances. As the theatre was a much frequented place different decrees and acts, such as manumissions, are carved on its walls.

The east entrance (parodos) to the theatre leads to the remaining monuments of the sanctuary. These consist of two unidentified treasuries **(93-94)** and the remains of an archaic building, the Poteidanion **(95)**.

Reconstruction of the Krateros votive offering (F. Courby).
Opposite: Theatre. Behind, the Phaidriades.

The Stadium

A full tour of Delphi should include a visit to the stadium, although the path up from the theatre is steep and takes time. Halfway up the ancient spring of *Kerna* can be seen and the niches for offerings cut in the rock around it.

The first stadium was built in the 5th century BC, as can be ascertained from an inscription built into its south wall. Initially there were no seats for the audience and the seats of stone from Parnassos (not marble as Pausanias says) were paid for by Herodes Atticus in the time of Hadrian. Four bulky pillars in the entrance supported three arches; there were niches for statues in the two central ones. The beginning and end of the track are marked by two rows of oblong slabs with notches for the runners's feet at the start and with square holes for the posts which divided the competitors. The length was about 178 m (the Pythian stade was exactly 178.35 m, the Roman 177.55 m) and the width about 25.50 m. The two long sides of seats are united by the curved end of the stadium and are separated from the track by a small podium 1.30 m

The Stadium. In front, remains of built piers that carried the triple arches of the entrance. Opposite: general view of the Stadium. The uphill path from the Theatre to the Stadium entrance can be seen.

high, which is composed of a foundation course, upright blocks and katalepter (a course along the top). Circulation was facilitated by stairs at the east ends of the long sides and at the curved end and by others which divided the rows of seats, as well as a gangway all round above the seats. There are twelve rows of seats on the north side, where the landscape is suitable, and one with a backrest, and six rows on the south side; they accommodated about 7000 spectators. In the middle of the north side is a long bench with a backrest which replaces two rows of seats. This is the seat for the judges and other important people. There is a fountain with an arch above it at the northwest end for the thirsty audience. In 1971 fragments of Doric architectural pieces from a 6th century fountain, which bad been there before the stadium, were found in its Roman debris.

Decorative details of the mosaic floor of the 5th c. AD. Early Christian basilica, which is exhibited outside the Museum.

THE MUSEUM

The Museum of Delphi contains one of the finest collections of original ancient Greek art in the world.

The archaeological finds in the exhibition complete the picture formed by the visitor of the archaeological site and are valuable evidence for the development of the art and pursuits of every period, showing the changes in the site from prehistoric to Early Christian times. Virtually all the rooms contain exhibits of paramount importance which hold the visitor's fixed attention, like the outstanding examples of sculpture, capped by the unique masterpiece of the Charioteer.

The principal theme of the display on the first floor is the history of the Delphic Sanctuary and the Oracle, and the finds are displayed as far as possible according to chronological and thematic units.

Several of the rooms are devoted to a group or groups of finds from a common provenance, for example from the Temple of Apollo, the Treasury of the Athenians or the Tholos in the Sanctuary of Athena Pronaia, etc.

The finds on the ground floor come from the city of Delphi and its cemeteries, and in the Museum enclosure there are architectural members, statue bases, funerary monuments and a host of inscriptions and mosaics, which complement the picture of the site of Delphi.

There is also a mosaic floor from a 5th c. AD basilica outside the Museum, with animals and two men holding baskets of fruit, symbolising the months of the year.

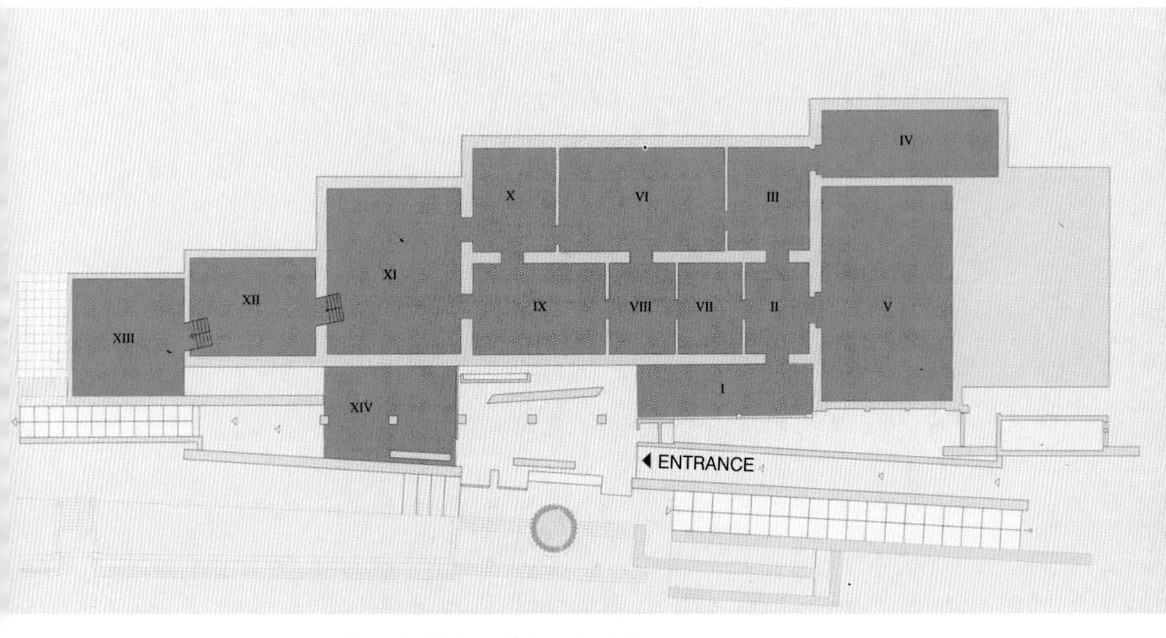

Plan of 1st floor of the Delphi Museum.

Rooms I-II: The beginnings of the sanctuary and the early offerings

In the first room of the Delphi Museum are assembled important finds illustrating the beginnings of the Delphic Sanctuary.

Case 1 contains the earliest exhibits, including fragments of Minoan rhytons, one in the form of a lion's head, and clay Mycenaean animal and female figurines, probably deities which were worshipped at the site before Apollo.

They are followed by fragments of bronze tripods and their decorative components, like cauldrons, sirens, handles, two anthropomorphic figurines and many busts of gryphons, dating to the Geometric period (900-700 BC).

One example is the iron tripod **(9467)** with feet in the shape of bulls' hooves. It recalls the tripod in the adyton of the temple, which had a cauldron for incense on top of it. There were many other similar votive offerings in the Sanctuary of Apollo. The cauldron in the Museum exhibit does not in fact belong with the tripod, nor is it of the same date or style, but has been included in order to complete the display.

In **Case 2** are three bronze shields and objects imported from Crete, Cyprus and the East. One of the shields is decorated with embossed concentric circles interrupted by two lines in the form of a V. This type of shield has been given the name Herzsprung. Similar shields exist in Greece (Cyprus, Rhodes, Crete), and also the in Iberian peninsula, Ireland and North Europe, which have a U shape instead of the V. The example from Delphi is dated to the 1st half of the 7th c. BC and was a votive offering in the Sanctuary of Apollo. The other two shields are decorated with the embossed bust of a lion with other animals incised around it, like lions, rams, roe deer, etc. Two figures can be seen between the legs of the lion on one of the two shields.

Among the 7th c. objects imported from Crete and Cyprus may be singled out the stand for a cauldron from Crete depicting a stag; the lower part of a lion's leg formed one of the supports of its bronze tripod and carries an inscription in the Cypriot syllabic script.

The 7th c. BC Palm Bowl with embossed scenes of a city siege and the Sirens from Syria were also imports from the East.

Lastly, **Case 3** contains figurines of bronze male figures, which were individual votive offerings in the Sanctuary of Apollo.

In the second room there are two **cases** with bronze figurines, chiefly of horses, oxen and rams, some of which were dedicated as separate votive offerings, while others were ornaments attached to the shoulders of bronze cauldrons and tripods of the Geometric period (900-700 BC).

Next comes the marble base of a fountain basin (*perirrhanterion*) **(5733)** with three girls on the supporting column, the lower parts of which are restored in plaster. It dates to around the 1st quarter of the 6th c. BC.

In the two next cases are displayed clasps and pins of different types, buttons, amulets, bronze helmets of Corinthian type (7th-6th c. BC) and votive weapons like spear– and arrowheads, pointed spear butts and Archaic and Classical axes.

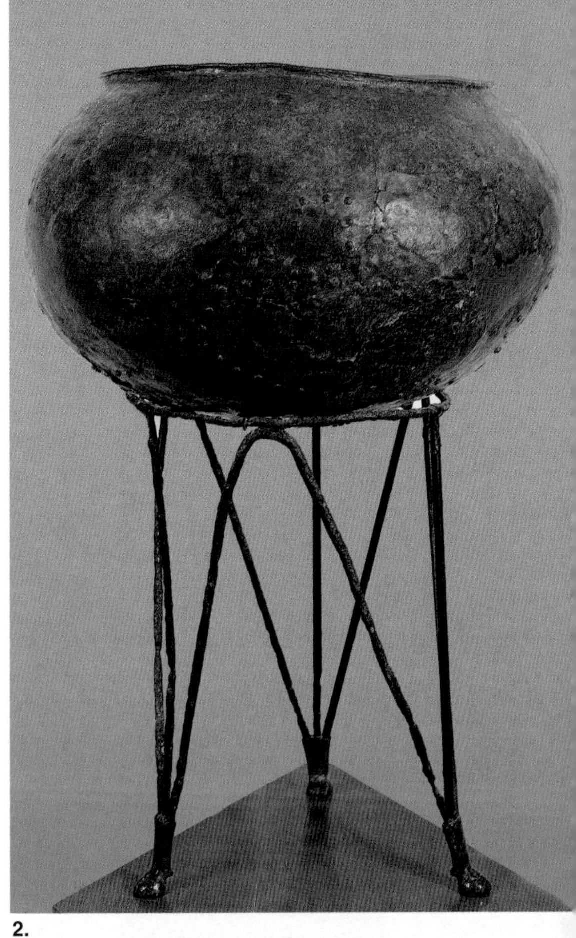

1. 2.

3.

1. Bronze griffin head.
2. Iron tripod.
3. Bronze siren from a lebes.

A small bronze kouros **(2527)**, 19 cm tall, possibly a statuette of Apollo, is also exhibited in a case. It is thought to be of Cretan workmanship of the Middle Daedalic period, in the second half of the 7th c. BC.

Bronze "daedalic" statuette.

Bronze shield.

Room III: The early archaic period

This room is dominated by two Archaic kouroi standing beside each other, masterpieces of the Doric art of the Peloponnese and outstanding for their high artistry and historical importance.

We know both their names and that of their sculptor. They were Cleobis and Biton, and the artist who made them was Polymedes from Argos, as the inscription on the plinth tells us.

Herodotus (1.31) has preserved the story for us. The Athenian Solon, one of the seven sages of Greece, was being entertained by Croesus at Sardis. He was shown the great riches of the Lydian king and afterwards Croesus asked him whom he thought was the richest and happiest person in the world. Solon said, Tellus the Athenian. When he was asked a second time, he mentioned Cleobis and Biton. They were Argives and well endowed with both wealth and health. When the time came for the festival of Hera, their mother, who was a priestess of Hera, had to go from Argos up to the temple, but the oxen were late in returning from the fields, so her two sons took their place and hauled the wagon with their mother to the Heraion, 8 kilometers away. They were the praise of everyone and their priestess mother prayed to Hera to reward her children in the best possible way. The boys then went to sleep in the Sanctuary, but never woke up. And the

◀ *Archaic Kouroi: Cleobis and Biton.*

Metope from the monopteral treasury of the Sikyonians. ▶

Wild boar on a metope from the monopteral treasury of the Sikyonians. ▼

Argives dedicated statues of them at Delphi, for being “the best of mortals”, in the words of Herodotus.

The statues, 2.16 m high, are among the earliest known kouroi, dating to around 570-560 BC. Scholars detect in these two statues, masked by the immobility of their pose, the virtuous qualities conveyed by the inner tension of their faces. Cleobis and Biton do not have the action of a discus thrower, but the interior, invisible movement of their bodies and the intensity of their expressions show how they anticipate the step towards the perfection of Classical art that followed.

Recently, however, the identification of the statues has been doubted and some scholars believe they represent the Dioscuri, who were worshipped in Laconia.

Also of interest are the metopes of the poros stone monopteral votive offering of the Sikyonians (no. 16 on the plan), which date to around 560 BC. They are unusually long (88 x 58 cm). Only five of them survive and they are badly preserved, but traces of paint are still visible and some details are incised.

The first metope takes its theme from the expedition of the Argonauts. The second depicts the abduction of Europa by Zeus transformed into a bull. The third is the best preserved and shows Castor and Polydeuces and their cousins Ida and Lynceus in a variation of the myth of the cattle stealing in Arcadia. The fourth metope shows a scene from the hunting of the Calydonian

Odysseus tied beneath the ram.

Boar, and the fifth preserves part of a representation of the story of the Golden Fleece, which Phryxus carried off riding on the ram.

Parts of the terracotta decoration of Archaic buildings, like simas, antefixes, etc., with fine designs and wonderfully preserved colours, are also displayed here.

Lastly, in the two **Cases** are displayed typical bronze sculptures of the Archaic period, like statuettes of kouroi or Apollo, sheet–metal plaques and utensils coverd with mythological scenes.

The bronze statuette of a kouros **(1663)** stands out, perhaps depicting Apollo (it is on temporary loan to the Museum of Ancient Olympia). It is naked, but wearing sandals on its feet and a necklace round its neck. The hair is held close to the head by a net, but fine ringlets hang down to the chest. It is considered a fine example of Laconian work of around 525 BC.

Mythological scenes cover the bronze relief plaque from the 2nd half of the 6th c. BC, showing Odysseus escaping from the Cyclops Polyphemus under a ram's belly, and the late 6th c. BC sheathing from an object with Heracles presenting the Erymanthian boar to Eurystheus, who is hiding in a jar.

Bronze Kouros – possibly representing Apollo.

Room IV: The sacred pits with gold-and-ivory objects

The excavation of the Sanctuary of Apollo was thought to be nearly completed, when in 1939, underneath the paving of the Sacred Way, at a depth of only 20 cm two repositories were discovered filled with fragments of ivory, gold, silver, bronze, iron and terracotta mixed with charcoal and ashes.

The larger repository contained parts of three singular statues of natural size. In the second repository were the remains of a silver bull. The sacred remains had been buried during the 5th c. BC after a fire and were works of Ionian art, perhaps from Asia Minor.

In the centre of the **case**, one side is dominated by the parts of three ivory statues of the 6th c. BC probably depicting Apollo, his sister Artemis and their mother Leto.

The ivory statue of Apollo is displayed first, sitting on a throne. An attempt has been made to restore the ivory head of the god, with hair made of gilt sheet and two gold tresses hanging down on his chest. A fragment of the god's right hand,holding the silver gilt bowl is displayed. Part of the adornment of the god's clothing consisted the gold discs fixed to bronze plaques with hammered representations of rosettes. The gold bands with a rosette decoration and the gold sheets, each with eight hammered representations of an animal, decorated the fringes of the god's clothing. The ivory tips of the god's feet projected from under the garment. His gold diadem is also shown, with six added rosettes and tresses from the hair of the statues.

Next come the heads of the two female figures, each wearing a gold diadem. The head of Artemis has been restored with gold earrings in the form of rosettes on ivory. Of the statue of Artemis there survives an arm comprising two parts fitted together and the goddesses toes.

The largely destroyed head probably belongs to Leto. Gold ornaments, like the bracelets, a crescent-shaped ornament, a necklace with gold beads in the shape of lion's heads and the bracelets of gaiters adorned both figures.

The picture of the two statues was completed by the gold sheets with hammered depictions of gryphons and gorgons fixed to bronze plaques and the gold bands that formed part of the decoration of the garments, and lastly the ivory bands with gold appliqué rosettes.

It is one of the earliest exhibits in this room, dating to the 2nd half of the 7th c.BC, and represents a male deity, probably Apollo. It is an example of Asia Minor art with a strong Eastern influence and was made by a Greek artist.

The rest of the exhibits of miniature art from similar or other materials are displayed in groups. They consist of gold and bronze sheets, three terracotta female figures, parts of inlaid decoration from 6th c. BC furniture, for example ivory cut-out plaques, heads, hands and bare soles, and three similar heads from chryselephantine statuettes, a head and arms from 6th c. BC ivory statuettes, two pairs of feet with elaborate sandals belonging to smaller ivory statues of female figures and parts of ivory groups with relief cut-out figures. One group shows the Harpies (Aello and Ocypete) running to the right after stealing Phineas's food, as Zetes and Calaïs, the sons of Boreas, pursue them,

Ivory statuette of a god.

and the end of Phineas's hand, it is supposed, can be seen on a little table. It is considered a masterpiece of Corinthian miniature art dating to around 570 BC. Similar partly preserved ivory groups depict battles in the Trojan War. They come from the decoration of little chests.

There are ivory cut-out plaques or heads, hands and feet, and other ivory ornamental plaques adorned with meanders and rosettes, fragments of two ivory face-to-face bulls, a 6th c. BC work, and below, a Chimaira, a "lion before, serpent behind, she-goat in the middle". Gold bands and flowers, which formed part of the decoration. Also Ionian miniature art of the 6th c. BC is the group with relief cut-out ivory figures depicting the departure of a warrior in a chariot, perhaps Amphiaraos. Similar in style are the ivory groups with scenes of battle. The display also includes two gold flowers, little bronze shields and vase handles and iron spearheads.

Gold and ivory head, probably of Artemis. ▶

◀ *Head, probably of Apollo, made of ivory, silver and gold.*

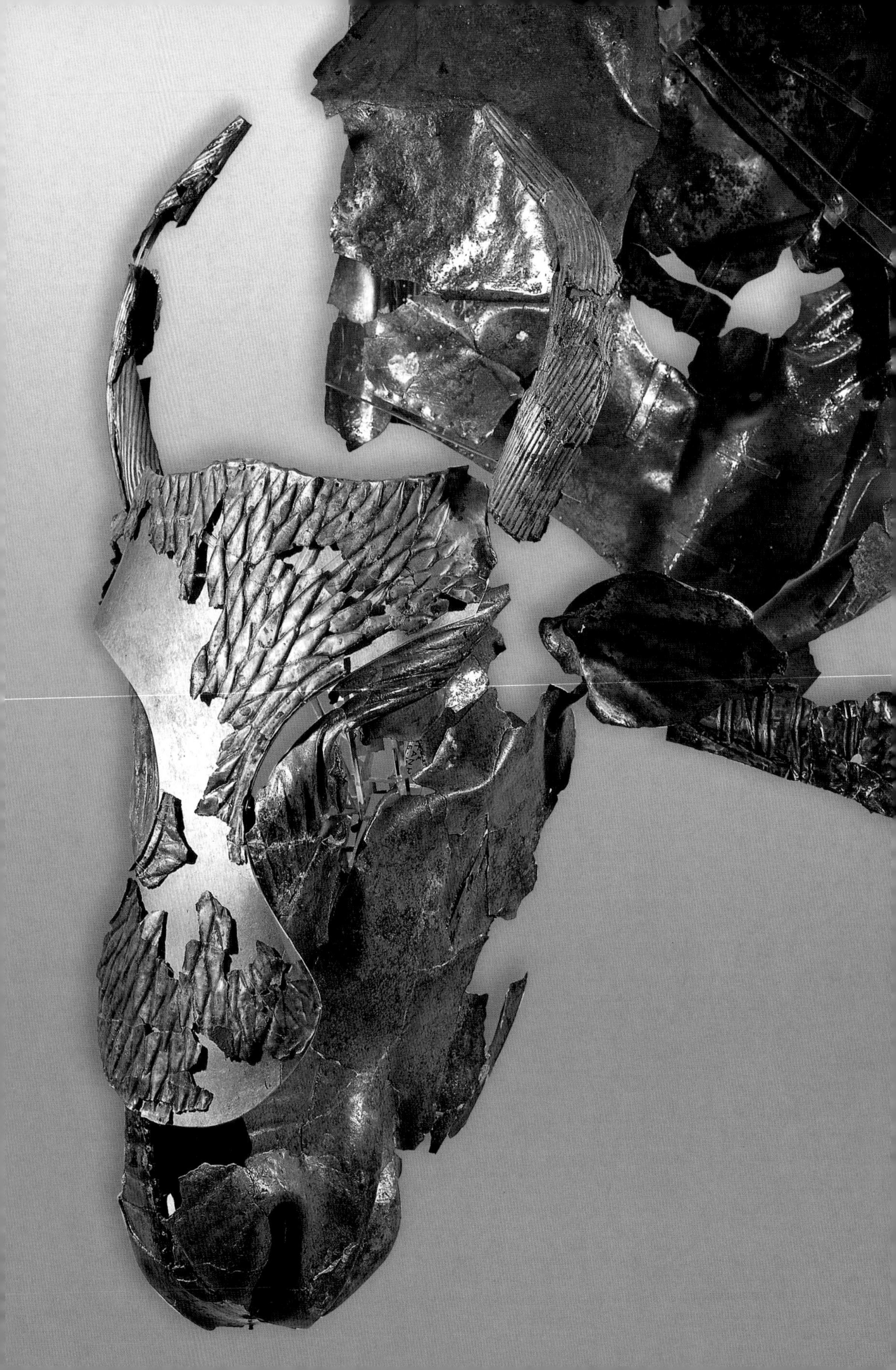

◀ The head of the silver Bull.

Gold sheet with a lively depiction of a griffin. ▶

Gold blossoms. ▼

On the other side is one of the most important exhibits, the silver statue of a bull. Its original dimensions were approximately 2.30 x 1.25 m, in other words it was life size **(10660)**. It was constructed of hammered silver sheets joined together by bronze bands and nailed with silver nails onto a wooden core. It is a wonderful work by Ionian artists of the 6th c. BC. In the 2nd half of the 5th c. BC it was destroyed by an unknown cause and piously buried in the repository of the Alo, where it was discovered in an unrecognisable condition. The restoration was carried out by craftsmen of the National Archaeological Museum of Athens.

Room V: The treasury of the Siphnians

This room contains rare masterpieces of Archaic art from the islands of the Aegean.

The visitor is first of all impressed by the colossal marble head of a Sphinx in the middle of the right-hand wall. This is the famous Sphinx of the Naxians, which was dedicated by the citizens of the island of Naxos in the Sanctuary of Apollo in about 560 BC (for the place of the votive offering on the site, see above n° 41). At this time Naxos, master of the Cyclades, was at its peak and tried to impose its control over the island of Delos as well, where the Naxians also dedicated another smaller Sphinx. The Sphinx of the Naxians dominated the site of the Sanctuary by the exotic appearance of the mythical beast erected on an Ionic base 12.10 m high, but also by its incomparable art. The Sphinx itself is 2.32 m high, bringing the total height of the monument to over 14.40 m. It has the head of a woman, like an Archaic kore with its characteristic smile, the breast and wings of a bird, and the body of a lion. The details were accentuated by the use of colour. Mythical figures of monsters came to Greece from the East, but a characteristic Greek touch was the humanizing of the figures by the harmonious combination of disparate elements and the smooth transition from animal and monster to human, seen in the wonderful head of the Sphinx.

To understand the meaning of the votive offering we must remember that the site of the age-old sanctuary of Ge was once guarded by Python, who was killed by Apollo. The gift of Naxos, the Sphinx, a daemon of Ge and the emblem of Naxos, had the meaning of guarding the Sacred place, as it was once guarded by Python. On the lower of the six drums of the column with its 44 shallow flutes, that is on the base of the offering, was engraved a decree of Delphi which restored the prerogative of prediction to the Naxians for the year 328/327 BC.

The sculptural decoration of the Treasury of the Siphnians has survived almost intact and occupies the largest part of the room. Herodotus (3.57) tells us that the Siphnians created one of the most sumptuous treasuries at Delphi (no. 19 on the plan of the site). It must have been completed in 525 BC when Samian fugitives plundered Siphnos, thus putting an end to its period of prosperity. The sculptures of the frieze appear to have been carved by at least two artists. The more conservative of them was the sculptor who made the carvings on the south

The Sphinx from Naxos.

and west sides of the treasury, who remained faithful to the Ionian tradition of the Asia Minor coast. The artist who carved the east and north sides facing the Sacred Way, seems to have been more inventive and influenced by a training in Chian workshops, but even more by Athenian art. All the sculptures were accentuated by the use of bright colours, traces of which are still visible. The ground was blue, and traces of red and green can be detected on the clothing and hair of the figures and the shields of the warriors. Many weapons had parts of inlaid bronze and many figures had their names painted.

The **East Frieze** depicts the Trojan War (right) watched by the gods of Olympus (left). The seated gods are divided into Greek and Trojan supporters. On the left are those friendly to Troy: Ares in armour by himself at the end, Aphrodite (or Leto) talking to Artemis and Apollo, while Zeus (head missing) sits on a magnificent throne decorated with a Satyr chasing a nymph. On his right are the gods supporting the Greeks. Perhaps Thetis, Achilles' mother, is shown kneeling at Zeus' feet, as she prays to the almighty father of the gods. This section is missing except for parts of fingers resting on Zeus' knees. Poseidon (missing), Athena, Hera and Demeter (or Hebe) were shown on the right. The battle unfolds in the right-hand part of this side. A four-horse chariot driven by Glaucos belongs to the Trojans. Next Aeneas and Hector fight with Menelaus (with a gorgon head on his shield) and Ajax over the body of a dead warrior. the four-horse chariot on the right is Greek and driven by Automedon.

Siphnian treasury: Ares, Aphrodite, Artemis, Apollo, Zeus.

Nestor, both an able fighter and orator, stands in front of it, encouraging the Greeks with his raised right hand.

The **North Frieze** depicts a Gigantomachy (battle between gods and giants). On the left Hephaistos at his forge fills his bellows with air to prepare his missiles. In front of him two goddesses fight two Giants. Further on the goddess Cybele stands in a chariot drawn by two impressive lions, which are mauling a Giant. Behind her Heracles in his lion skin can be seen fighting another Giant. On the right Apollo and Artemis shoot arrows at three Giants. Between them in the background the Giant Kantharos looking behind him runs in fear to the right,. On the crest of his helmet is his emblem, the kantharos, which is named after him. Further on Zeus was shown in his chariot (not preserved) fighting two Giants; his wife, Hera, stoops over a Giant she has struck down. Further to the right Athena is fighting the Giant Laertes. Another Giant has already fallen to the ground. Beyond, Ares is fighting two Giants and Hermes stabs two others with his spear. On the right side, restored in plaster, Poseidon and perhaps Amphitrite are battling two Giants. The sculptor wrote his name on the shield of the third of the Giants fighting Apollo and Artemis, but the inscription is worn and this superb sculptor remains unknown.

The **West Frieze**, on the front of the treasury, depicts the Judgment of Paris. According to the myth, Eris, goddess of Discord, was not invited to the wedding of Peleus and Thetis, so in order to avenge herself she threw an apple

1. Greeks and Trojans from the east frieze of the Siphnian treasury.
2. Gods and giants from the north frieze of the Siphnian treasury.

1. Gods and giants from the north frieze of the Siphnian treasury.
2. Section of Gigantomachy from the north frieze of the Siphnian treasury.

Detail of the north frieze of the Siphnian treasury: Apollo, Artemis and the Giant Kantharos.

Detail of the north frieze of the Siphnian treasury:
Hera stoops over a giant she has knocked to the ground.

among the guests inscribed "To the most beautiful". This led to a dispute between Hera, Athena and Aphrodite. Zeus appointed Paris as judge and he gave the apple to Aphrodite. In the frieze the story is divided into three parts, one for each goddess. On the left a winged Athena mounts her chariot drawn by winged horses driven by Hermes. A god behind her may be Hephaistos or Poseidon. In the centre of the frieze the winner, Aphrodite descends from her chariot, coquettishly fingering her necklace. She is the most beautiful figure in the whole Siphnian frieze. The third part, on the right, is not preserved, but it must have shown Hera with her chariot.

The **South Frieze** is known from only a few fragments and they are insufficient to reveal the subject. One of the pieces depicts the abduction of a female figure by an unidentified hero who is mounting a chariot (Pelops and Hippodameia, or the Dioscuri with the daughters of Leucippus). Another chariot is shown in front of an altar, and part of a third and two horses are also present.

Nothing has been found of the relief sculptures on the West Pediment, which means that either they have vanished or else that there never was any pedimental relief decoration on the side of the entrance, which would have been strange. There remain the sculptures on the East Pediment of the Treasury.

The representations on the East Pediment, which was 0.73 m high in the centre, are quite well preserved. This pediment is unusual in that the lower parts of the sculpture are in relief while the upper parts are in the round. It depicts the well known theme of the dispute between Heracles and Apollo over

Heracles' attempt to steal the tripod; east pediment of the Siphnian treasury.

the possession of the Delphic Tripod, a story also known from vase painting and other works of art. The myth has it that Heracles, enraged because the Pythia refused him an oracle on the grounds that he had not been purified after the murder of Iphitus, seized the prophetic tripod with the intention of founding his own oracle. On the pediment the two gods are shown tugging at the tripod, Heracles to the right and Apollo to the left, while in the middle a taller divine figure, once thought to be Athena or Zeus, but nowadays Hermes, tries to separate the two quarrelers. Behind Apollo, his sister Artemis (or his mother Leto) are holding him back. Further to the left two female figures stand in front of a horse-drawn chariot whose charioteer is kneeling in the left corner. At the right end of the pediment is another chariot after two figures, etc.

One of the two Caryatids from the sculptural decoration is also exhibited. These figures supported the entablature of the facade of the Treasury of the Siphnians instead of columns. Most of the torso has survived, as well as the head wearing a polos, on top of which rested the capital (displayed on a separate base), which is embellished with two lions attacking a stag. The height of the column was completed by the lower part of the torso and the high base. Holes in the hair and diadem of the Caryatid indicate that the beauty of the lovely kore was originally enhanced by metal ornaments. She is dressed in a thin chiton and over it a short himation with a thickly folded overfall. Sileni and Maenads are depicted in relief on the polos (or *kalathos*).

In antiquity the magnificent doorframe at the entrance to the cella would have been visible between the two Caryatids at the back of the pronaos of the Treasury of the Siphnians. It was adorned with relief rosettes, lotus blossoms and other flowers, like the better preserved entrance to the Erechtheion. The Siphnian Caryatids were in fact the forerunners of the Caryatids of the Erechtheion on the Acropolis at Athens.

Also on show are parts of the roof of the treasury, one section decorated with relief palmettes and lotuses, and another with a lion's head in the middle which served as a rainspout on the roof. Also:

The body of a Caryatid **(1526, 3611[a])**, which probably came from the Treasury of the Cnidians and dates to the mid 6th c. BC.

The head of a Caryatid with a cylindrical polos (cap) **(1203)**, on which is depicted in relief Apollo Kitharodos (lyre player), while beside him stand four Nymphs and in front the Three Charites with Hermes playing a pipe. It belonged to an unknown treasury, but was previously ascribed to the facade

Four–horse chariot in front of an altar, from the south frieze of the Siphnian treasury.

Caryatid from the facade of the Siphnian treasury.

Head of a Caryatid with a cylindrical polos.

of the Treasury of the Cnidians. A work of Ionian style, perhaps from the Chios school. Ca. 530 BC.

A small Ionic column **(997, 3424)** of Parian marble, a votive offering of the sons of Charopinos, like the inscribed base **(2278)** with the plinth and feet of a kouros. Mid 6th c. BC.

Two fine exhibits can be seen in the torsos of two kouroi of Parian marble. One **(2557)** dates to around 540-520 BC, and the other **(2696)** to 555-540 BC.

Room VI: The temple of Apollo

This room contains the pedimental sculptures from the Temple of Apollo belonging to two different building phases.

From the Archaic temple, known as the temple of the Alcmeonids, come sculptures from the two pediments and architectural members. The room is dominated by the sculptures from the marble pediment at the east end of the temple, showing the "epiphany" of the god Apollo at Delphi. He appears in a frontal four-horse chariot occupying the centre of the scene. He is accompanied, it has been suggested, by his mother, Leto, and sister, Artemis. There are three male and female figures respectively on either side. On the right Delphos, who is considered the lord of the place, receives the god, and two other male figures, while on the left three female figures, perhaps the daughters of Cecrops, the king of the Athenians.

The two corners of the pediment are filled with animal groups: in the right corner a lion attacks a stag, and in the left a lion brings down a bull.

Surviving traces of paint indicate that the lions' manes, the blood from the wounds and the fringes of the garments were painted red, and other details would also have been picked out in colour.

The west poros pediment depicts a Gigantomachy. Athena attacking a fallen Giant, a male figure and the fore parts of two horses have survived.

They are supposed to be works by the famous Athenian sculptor Antenor, and the preserved fragments are certainly worthy of his reputation.

The display of the sculpture from the Archaic temple is completed by the central acroterion of the temple, the marble winged Nike and the marble lion's head rainspout.

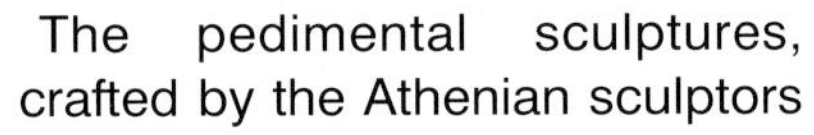

The pedimental sculptures, crafted by the Athenian sculptors Praxias and Androsthenes, are from the 4th c. BC temple. The east pediment shows Apollo with Leto, Artemis and the Muses, and the west one Dionysos as Dionysos Kitharodos between the Thyiades (Maenads).

Part of a rainspout **(8198)** from the architectural members of this temple is also on display.

Reconstruction of the capital and base of an Ionic column from the interior colonnade of the 4th c. BC Temple of Apollo.

Winged Victory, an akroterion from the temple of the Alcmaeonids.

Dionysos, from the west pediment of the temple.

Rooms VII-VIII: The treasury of the Athenians

The Rooms of the Treasury of the Athenians contain the 24 best preserved metopes from the Treasury (n° 30 on the plan). There were 30 metopes in all, six on the ends and nine on the sides. The metopes on the facade show scenes of an Amazonomachy. Those on the north and west sides have a common theme: the Labours of Heracles. The more celebrated south side, better viewed from the Sacred Way, was reserved for the Exploits of Theseus, the Athenian national hero and founder of Athens, who united the inhabitants of Attica.

The artists who worked on the metopes have been separated into two groups, one more conservative, and another who opened the way from the Late Archaic to the Early Classical period in Attic sculpture.

The acroteria and parts of the pedimental sculptures are exhibited in a case in the room next to that of the Treasury of the Athenians. The subject of the east pediment was the meeting of two heroes, possibly Theseus and Peirithous, king of the Lapiths, and the west one depicted a battle featuring Heracles.

A uniquely singular exhibit in this room is the fragments of hymns to Apollo, which were incised (138 and 128 BC) on the south wall of the Treasury together with the notes for the choral singing on the upper part and for the instrumental music on the lower. The notes have been deciphered by Fr. Bellermann and K. Fortlage.

Parts of a hymn to Apollo from the Athenian treasury.

Theseus and an Amazon, on a metope from the Athenian treasury.

Heracles killing the Kerynian stag; metope from the Athenian treasury.

Clay kylix depicting Apollo.

Apollo pouring a libation, from the interior of the kylix.

In the next **Case** are bronze votive utensils of the 6th-5th c. BC with mainly ritual functions.

One of the **Cases** contains the most beautiful of the clay finds at Delphi. This is the white lekythos **(8140)** with a unique representation of Apollo, dating to the years 480-470 BC, the period of the Severe Style. The ancient potter drew Apollo with fine brown lines, sitting on a folding stool with legs ending in lions' feet. He wears a sleeveless chiton fastened at the shoulders. His back and lower body is wrapped in a purple himation. His hair and the wreath of myrtle leaves are golden. His right hand pours a libation of wine from a bowl and his left one holds a seven-string lyre, which he plucks with his fingers. The sound box of the lyre is made from the shell of a tortoise. A black bird is perched enquiringly in front of his face. The bird's colour makes it probable it is a crow and it symbolises Coronis, the beautiful daughter of King Phlegyas, whom Apollo loved.

Room IX: Votive offerings of the 5th c. BC

This room contains typical examples of 5th c. BC art.

The bronze statuettes in the centre, important for our knowledge of 5th c. BC bronze work, were found in two repositories in the Sacred Way. They include a bronze incense burner **(7723)** held by a female figure wearing a peplos above her head. The incense burner has the shape of a hemispherical cauldron, in which the incense was placed and covered with a perforated lid. It is a masterpiece of Parian work, ca. 450 BC.

The bronze group of athletes **(7722)** on a common base shows an athlete with jumping weights and a wreath, together with an umpire, who appears to be declaring him the winner, from an Attic workshop, ca. 460 BC, and a bronze figurine of a piper-player **(7724)**, dating to the beginning of the 5th c. BC.

An Aeolian capital from the Treasury of Massalia, dating to ca. 540-500 BC, stands at one side of the room.

The limestone head of a female figure is of special interest as it preserves its original white and red paint and comes from the pedimental sculptures of the temple of Athena Pronaia, which is dated to the end of the 6th c.BC.

In a **case** beyond are fragments of the sculptural decoration of the Treasury of Massalia, dating to ca. 500 BC, and of the Doric Treasury, which dates to ca. 470 BC. The female and male figures from the Treasury of Massalia formed part of a composition which probably depicted an Amazonomachy or Gigantomachy.

Next come five statues of kores full of life and movement, and acroteria from unidentified buildings in the Sanctuary of the Pronaia, like the female statue **(4780)**, which probably formed an acroterion on the Doric Treasury in the Sanctuary of Athena Pronaia dating to 480-470 BC.

The next group consists of polychrome terracotta architectural members

Bronze incense–burner. ▶

Bronze statuette of a pipe–player.

Bronze statuette of a cow. ▼

from monuments on the site: notable are the simas, the antefixes from different buildings and the acroteria from the temple of Athena Pronaia.

In another **case** are displayed a bronze statuette of a cow and parts of large bronze statues, fine examples of the large bronze statuary of the Classical period.

Room X: The tholos of the sanctuary of Athena Pronaia

This room contains parts of the sculptured decoration and architectural members of the Tholos, the circular building in the Sanctuary of Athena Pronaia.

The principal decoration of the Tholos was two Doric friezes of Parian marble, one larger than the other.

The larger one was on the outside above the external colonnade and architrave, as we can see better in the partially restored replica of the Tholos at the site of the Sanctuary of Pronaia. The metopes on the frieze measure 65 x 62.5 cm and depict scenes of Amazonomachies and Centauromachies.

Part of the entablature of the Tholos with four of the exterior metopes can be seen restored in the room.

The small frieze adorned the upper part of the wall of the Tholos on the outside with metopes measuring 42 x 40.5 cm showing the exploits of the two greatest mythical heroes of the Greeks, Heracles and Theseus.

The sculptures from the Tholos of male and female figures exhibited in the cases date to around 380 BC. They are very fine works by artists in high relief and display a boldness and freedom of movement and the dramatic tension of action, combined with nobility of line and form.

The Roman architect Vitruvius mentions Theodoros from Phocaia as the architect of the Tholos. The French archaeologist J. Marcadé noticed similarities between the sculptures of the Tholos and those of the Asclepeion at Epidaurus and maintained that the Theodoros of the Tholos at Delphi was the same artist referred to in the building inscriptions on the Temple of Asclepius at Epidaurus.

The picture of the Tholos is filled out by one of the Doric capitals of the exterior colonnade, by a Corinthian half-column from the interior colonnade and the female statues that formed the acroteria of the Tholos.

Room XI: The late classical - hellenistic period

This room contains exhibits of great importance for the history both of the Sanctuary and of Classical and Hellenistic art.

It includes the multifigural family votive offering of Daochos II from Pharsala, who in the years 338-334 BC was the tetrarch of Thessaly and a *hieromnemon* (religious official) of Thessaly at the Amphictionic Assembly of Delphi and president of the Assembly. We have seen the site of the votive offering in the Sanctuary of Apollo (n° 70 on the map). The inscriptions in verse on the plinth celebrate the political, athletic and military achievements of members of this Thessalian family of Daochos.

There are spaces on the plinth for nine marble statues. Six were Daochos' ancestors (Aknonios, Agias, Telemachos, Agelaos, Daochos I and Sisyphos I), one was the dedicator himself, Daochos II, one was the son of Sisyphos II, and the last was for the god Apollo, whose statue has not survived. The god must have been sitting on a rock or on the Omphalos, as we see him depicted on the Delphic coins, and his statue was set on the right-hand end of the plinth. After him, in genealogical order came Aknonios, then the others and lastly Sisyphos II. In the reconstruction of the monument we see, from right to left, first Apollo's empty place, followed by Aknonios fully clothed, three naked athletes, namely the pancratiast Agias, the wrestler Telemachos and the runner Agelaos, and then Daochos I and Sisyphos I, clothed. Next came the dedicator himself, Daochos II, also clothed, and lastly the dedicator's son, Sisyphos II, leaning on a stele. In the place of Daochos II there is now only the plinth, and Telemachos is the torso of the athlete **(1360)** who was afterwards linked to the votive offering of Daochos.

In the same room there is a marble acanthus column with three dancers on the top. It was erected after the catastrophic earthquake of 373 BC. An inscription on the surviving fragments of the base tells us that it was a votive offering of the Athenians and it dates to 332-322 BC. The column, some 13 m high overall, was conspicuous not only for its height, but because of its exotic subject and its craftsmanship (n° 72 on the plan). The lowest drum has survived and the peculiar acanthus capital, on top of which the three dancers stand. They are dressed in diaphanous, high girdled, short chitons reaching to their knees. The smooth flesh shows through the garment. Over two metres tall, their left hands hold their chitons, while the right are raised in the movement of the dance; they wear polos caps on their heads. Recent study has shown that the Omphalos also belonged to this monument.

The marble Omphalos **(8194)**, the Delphic symbol par excellence, was covered by the *agrenon*, a net of woolen fillets carved in relief that was placed over an Omphalos.

In Classical times it symbolised the centre of the earth, for it was here at Delphi that the two eagles Zeus had loosed at the ends of the world met. In addition, the oval shape of the Omphalos had the form of a burial mound, which according to tradition concealed the bones of the god Dionysos or the dragon Python, which had been buried near the primeval oracle of its mother, Ge.

Sisyphos I, father of Daochos II.

The pancratiast, Agias.

The "dancing girls" from the column with the acanthus.

Next there are statues of children that were dedicated to the god Apollo, for example the charming marble statue of a girl dressed in a thick chiton **(1791)**. It resembles the votive offerings of little girls in the temples of Artemis Brauronia and Eileithyia and dates to the beginning of the 3rd c. BC.

4755: the marble statue of a boy holding a goose, a dedication to Apollo from the end of the 3rd c. BC. A Hellenistic marble statue of a young Eros.

On the south side of the room another multifigural votive offering comprises a female statue, a male statue of the Dionysos type usual in the period of the Severe Style, and the marble statue of an old man of the middle class. The offering, whose dedicator is mentioned as a "craftsman" of Dionysos, or a donor, dates to around 300 BC.

The marble statues of a young girl and a naked male figure wearing a chlamys **(1793)** may have belonged to the same votive offering.

Also on show are a marble statue of a seated figure **(823)**, perhaps Apollo, 4th c. BC, and a headless marble statue **(1876)** representing Apollo Kitharodos in the usual early Hellenistic style, beginning of 3rd c. BC.

The marble Omphalos (decorated with "agrenon").

Marble statuette of a girl.

Marble portrait of an old man.

Room XII: The late hellenistic - roman period

Late Hellenistic and in particular Roman sculptures are displayed here.

The circular marble altar, 1.076 m high, nearly in the centre of the room comes from the Sanctuary of Athena Pronaia, where it was found shattered in pieces. On the relief frieze twelve maidens in pairs are hanging festoons of ribbons. It is a 2nd c. BC work and is thought to have been in the Tholos or else in the open air for the worship of earth deities.

An exhibit of outstanding historical and artistic value is the frieze on the monument of Aemilius Paullus (n° 53 on the plan), depicting the battle of Pydna (22 June 168 BC) between the Romans and the Macedonians.

The inscription about Aemilius Paullus reads: L. Aemilius, L.f. inperator de rege Perse macedonibusque cepet.

One of the finest cult statues of Antinoos is displayed in this room. The young man from Bithynia in Asia Minor, famed for his beauty and the favourite of the emperor Hadrian, accompanied the emperor to the Nile, where he drowned in 130 BC.

Marble altar from the temple of Pronaia.

◀ *Marble statue of Antinoos.*

Detail of the statue of Antinoos. ▶

According to the myth surrounding his death, he gave his life for the emperor.

Hadrian proclaimed his deification in numerous places, and in Egypt he founded the city of Antinoopolis. Elsewhere Antinoos was honoured with festivities and the erection of statues. At Delphi he was portrayed as a god. The white smooth body contrasts with the lively movement of his hair, which is held by a band and would have been adorned with a gold wreath, as shown by the holes in the band. The black marble of the base further heightens the whiteness of the body.

It was an expression of the revival of romanticism during the 2nd c. AD, which manifests itself in both religion and art, with a tendency to revert to ancient Greek models. The marble is Parian and the sculptor must have been one of the finest exponents of his art in the decade of 130 AD.

Portrait head of an unknown man **(1706)**. It is thought to represent the Roman consul Titus Quintius Flamininus, who defeated Philip V of Macedonia in the battle of

Cynoscephalai (197 AD). It is an exceptional work of the beginning of the 2nd c. AD.

Characteristic examples of the art of portraiture can be seen in the two male portraits, one of them the mythical hero Heracles, which copy Classical originals and date to the time of the empire.

Next we have the frieze from the proscenium of the theatre with a relief representation of the Labours of Heracles **(2544)**, which should be dated to the 1st c. AD on the basis of the iconography and the monument's history. It was most probably made before Nero's visit in 67 AD with the aim of flattering the emperor.

The Latin inscription in large letters refers to repairs made to the temple under the emperor Domitian in 84 AD.

Room XIII: The Charioteer

This room houses one of the masterpieces of ancient Greek art, the Delphi Charioteer.

The Charioteer formed a part only of the votive offering, the whole of which included the four-horse chariot he was driving. The chariot hid the lower part of his body, which is why the upper part now appears disproportionately large.

In spite of the missing left arm and all the mishaps the statue suffered throughout the centuries, which have deprived it of its original lustre and some of the decorative details of the diadem, its state of preservation in general is admirable. Nothing of it has changed, and even the eyes are original, which is very rare.

Standing in front of the Charioteer with this in mind, and with the thrill of emotion the sight of his face inevitably rouses, let us glance back at its history.

The tyrants of Syracuse, the Deinomenids, are also known to us from the gold tripods they dedicated in the Sanctuary of Apollo (n° 65 on the plan) after their victory over the Carthaginians at Himera, and from the poems of Pindar and Bacchylides celebrating the victories at the Panhellenic Games. It is to one such victory at the Pythian Games that we owe the Charioteer. Polyzalos, one of the sons of Deinomenes, the tyrant of Gela, sent his chariot to Delphi and won at the Pythian Games in 478 or 474 AD. In his desire to perpetuate the memory of his victory, this devout and wealthy patron of the arts dedicated the bronze group to Apollo, according to the inscription on the partly preserved pedestal.

The group originally consisted of the chariot, the charioteer and, according to recent studies, two separate horses with their two grooms, either riding them or on foot. The picture of the offering is augmented by other bits of the bronze group, like parts of three horse's hooves, fragments of the chariot, pieces of the reins and the boy's right hand, which are displayed in the case.

Bearing this picture in mind, we turn back to the Charioteer. He is dressed in a long priestly chiton, customary for those taking part in a sacred ceremony. All the games in the great sanctuaries of antiquity had a religious character. The chiton is girdled high up with two straps. The heavy folds over his chest contrast with the fluted folds below the girdle. The same antithesis can be seen

◀ *Portrait, probably of T. Q. Flamininus.*

◀ *The Charioteer.*

Detail of the Charioteer. ▶

in the sprightly curls on his cheeks in contrast to the simple but carefully contrived movement of the curls on his head, which seem almost to be glued on. The diadem was the mark of his victory. The slight turning and inclination of the head and the shape of the face, with its flat cheeks contrasting with the intentionally full and asymmetrical chin and fleshy lips, are complemented by the "Greek profile" and crowned by the charioteer's gaze. The eyes, made of white enamel with black inset stones for the pupils and framed by the slightly slanting arched eyebrows, have been preserved intact.

We have before us a unique figure, a matchless masterpiece, eternal, but with an expression that betrays no emotion in the moment of the great victory. No instantaneous movement nor fleeting animation, only an immortal Olympian calm. Through his victory the mortal has become immortal, and the artist has succeeded in capturing his immortality. Who was the artist of the Charioteer, we don't know. The great artists in his time were Pythagoras the Samian and the slightly younger Kalamis, who worked in Athens. Nothing of their work has remained to us. It is to simple good fortune that we owe the Charioteer, which gives us some idea of the Greek sculpture of Classical times.

The Charioteer and his chariot lay for centuries buried by the rocks which tumbled down onto it in the earthquakes of 373 BC, to see the light of day once more with the French excavations in 1896 in a spot between the Theatre, the Offering of Krateros and the Ischegaon retaining wall.

Room XIV: The end of the sanctuary

In this room are exhibited finds which throw light on the changes that occurred in the Sanctuary with the transition from polytheism to Christianity and the demise of the Sanctuary.

The Herm **(4070)** carries the bust of the famous philosopher, biographer and for many years priest of Apollo, Plutarch (46-125 AD). The statue, as can be seen from the inscription, was a joint votive offering by the compatriots of Chaironeia and Delphi.

The portrait statue **(5667)** of an unknown philosopher of the imperial period is a good example of 2nd c. AD portrait sculpture. The philosopher's world is now enclosed within his mind. It was a world that was slowly dying, since it was no longer renewed by life, until the preaching of Jesus Christ arrived to annihilate it.

4040. Head of an elderly man in Pentelic marble, attributed to a Neoplatonic philosopher. His meditative, philosophical disposition and seriousness are apparent in his features. End of 4th c. AD.

Lastly, there is a specially interesting inscription with the letter of the emperor Claudius (41-54 AD) to the consul of Achaia, L. Junius Gallio, Seneca's brother. The inscription clearly reveals the emperor's interest in solving the acute problem which troubled the city of Delphi at that time, the shortage of citizens. The inscription also makes an important contribution to biblical history, for it helps to date the second of St Paul's missionary journeys. According to the Acts of the Apostles, L. Junius Gallio was acting as consul of Achaia at the time Paul stayed in Corinth.

Portrait of a philosopher – possibly representig Plutarch.